Otis Frederick Reed Waite

Claremont war History

April, 1861, to April, 1865...

Otis Frederick Reed Waite

Claremont war History
April, 1861, to April, 1865...

ISBN/EAN: 9783337010737

Printed in Europe, USA, Canada, Australia, Japan

Cover: Foto ©ninafisch / pixelio.de

More available books at **www.hansebooks.com**

CLAREMONT

WAR HISTORY;

APRIL, 1861, TO APRIL, 1865:

WITH SKETCHES OF

NEW-HAMPSHIRE REGIMENTS,

AND A

BIOGRAPHICAL NOTICE OF EACH CLAREMONT SOLDIER, ETC.

BY OTIS F. R. WAITE.

CONCORD:
McFARLAND & JENKS, PRINTERS.
1868.

Entered according to act of Congress, in the year 1868, by
OTIS F. R. WAITE,
In the Clerk's Office of the District Court of New-Hampshire.

PREFACE.

In preparing a book like this for the press there are many difficulties and embarrassments to be overcome. Where so many men are concerned who were influenced by similar motives of patriotism or reward, and experienced like hardships in battle, in camp, and in hospital, it is difficult to say much in praise of the acts of one without seeming to do injustice to others. It has been the desire of the author to do exact justice to all who took their lives in their hands, turned their backs upon families, friends, and home comforts, and for love of country and her institutions and laws, went forth to encounter all the dangers and hardships incident to the life of a soldier in time of war. If he has failed in this it has been for want of facts connected with many—notices of whom are brief—for the reason that themselves or friends neglected frequent appeals to furnish him with such material as it was impossible to obtain from other sources, and not on account of any feeling of partiality on his part. It has been the author's aim to withhold any encomiums of his own, and let each man's record speak for him.

PREFACE.

If notices of commissioned officers, as a class, seem more extensive than those of privates, it is because they occupied more conspicuous positions, and, in the nature of things, had a more varied experience, rather than because they exhibited more true patriotism in offering their services to the country, fought more bravely and nobly, were more faithful in the performance of every duty, or endured the privations pertaining to the life of a soldier with more uncomplaining patience. The privates in battle occupied positions of greatest danger, and fought with the same patriotic zeal as the officers; and, more than they, faced storms and cold, endured hardships and fatigue, suffered hunger and thirst, and battled disease and death in almost every shape, without a murmur or complaint. To the private soldiers belong a large share of the glorious results of the war. It would be vain to attempt to do justice to them and their self-sacrificing, heroic deeds.

If the following pages but contain an impartial and accurate record of the participation of the people of Claremont in the War of the Rebellion; convey a correct idea of their spirit and feeling, and a just account of the action of her soldiers in the field, the author has hit the mark he aimed at, and his ambition is fully satisfied.

O. F. R. W.

Claremont, N. H., 1868.

GENERAL INDEX.

	PAGE.
First Regiment,	41
Second Regiment,	45
Third Regiment,	73
Fourth Regiment,	93
Fifth Regiment,	95
Sixth Regiment,	147
Seventh Regiment,	157
Eighth Regiment,	165
Ninth Regiment,	167
Tenth Regiment,	181
Eleventh Regiment,	185
Twelfth Regiment,	189
Thirteenth Regiment,	191
Fourteenth Regiment,	193
Fifteenth Regiment,	209
Sixteenth Regiment,	211
Seventeenth Regiment,	213
Eighteenth Regiment,	215
New-Hampshire Cavalry,	217
First Light Battery,	233

GENERAL INDEX.

Heavy Artillery,	235
Sharp-shooters,	241
Vermont Ninth Regiment,	253
Other Vermont Regiments,	261
Massachusetts Regiments,	269
Regiments from other States,	277
Navy,	285
Summary,	290
Claremont's Quota,	291
Ladies' Soldiers' Aid Societies,	291
Thanksgiving,	298
Soldiers' Monument,	299

BIOGRAPHICAL INDEX.

A

	PAGE.
Abbott, Alba D.	76
Abbott, Charles S.	100
Adams, Jeffrey T.	283
Ainsworth, James E.	277
Alexander, Daniel S.	76
Allen, Heman	49
Allen, Charles S.	222
Allen, Oscar C.	48
Austin, William P.	243
Austin, Ruel G.	101
Austin, Albert J.	75
Ayer, Henry G.	221

B.

	PAGE.
Ballou, Charles O.	105
Ballou, Ethan A.	222
Bacon, Charles H.	101
Barker, Fred. L.	196
Bardwell, Charles R.	263
Bascom, James P.	169
Barnard, John P. W.	76
Benton, Samuel O.	103
Bigley, William H.	76
Bingham, C. Edward	277
Blanchard, Henry S.	263
Bolio, Horace	104
Bolio, Frank	102
Bowker, Charles S.	196
Bowler, John	196
Bowman, Selwin R.	107
Bond, Oliver A.	269
Booth, Oscar	236
Bradford, Amos F.	170
Bradford, Caleb M. D.	170
Bradford, David H.	170
Bradford, Hosea B.	170
Briggs, William H.	223
Brown, Albert W.	103
Brown, George E.	103
Brown, Josiah S.	104
Brown, Ralph N.	104
Brown, Hollis S.	104
Brough, Charles D.	107
Burns, James	102
Burns, Thomas	102
Burbank, Asher S.	261
Burrill, Alfred W.	182

Burrill, Charles F. . 103
Butcher, John . . 105

C.

Carleton, Elijah S. . 113
Carleton, Samuel S. . 269
Carroll, Charles . . 77
Chase, Luther A. . . 108
Chase, Robert Henry . 110
Chaffin, William Henry 197
Chaffin, Alvaro L. . 236
Chapman, Samuel W. . 271
Chandler, Selden S. . 49
Cheney, Ira D. . . 112
Clark, Francis . . 223
Clement, Wyman R. . 50
Colburn, Sanford . . 77
Colby, George . . 278
Colby, Gilbert F. . . 236
Colston, Charles F. . 114
Cone, Lyman H. . . 113
Cook, James A. . 49
Cook, Wendell R. . 108
Cook, Horace W. . 271
Cook, William W. . 108
Cooper, Sherman . 150
Crafts, Homer M. . 50
Craig, Joseph . . 109
Crowther, Samuel . 109
Cummings, Daniel . 113
Currier, George W. . 171

D.

Dane, Albert G. . 77
Dane, Wallace . . 264
Davis, George W. . 255
Davis, John W. . . 54
Davis, Ziba L. . . 53

Dean, John . . . 51
Delmage, James . 114
Dickey, Joseph A. . 200
Dooley, William . 159
Douglass, Jerome B. . 78
Dutton, Henry L. . 264
Dutton, Newell T. . 171

E.

Emerson, George W. . 78
Emerson, George H. 94
Evans, Frank W. . 78

F.

Fairbanks, George W. . 114
Farwell, William H. . 223
Fitch, George W. . . 288
Ford, Charles P. . 280
Ford, George E. . . 236
Ford, James B. . 279
Foster, Charles E. . 200
Freeman, Henry V. . 192
French, Edward E. . 246

G.

Garfield, Moses . . 160
Gardiner, Alexander . 200
Gates, James S. A. . 115
Germarsh, Israel . 115
Gilbert, John . . 79
Giles, Ethan A. . 264
Giles, Lemuel A. . . 115
Gillingham, Oliver P. 206
Goddard, Frederick W. 272
Gould, Warren H. . 237
Gowdey, Edwin M. . 54
Grandy, Charles B. . 280
Grannis, David H. 79

BIOGRAPHICAL INDEX.

Grannis, Timothy . 247
Grinnels, Chester F. . 115

H.
Hadley, Charles L. . 153
Hadley, William H. . 153
Hall, Levi D., Jr. . 206
Hall, Tracy L. . . 80
Hall, Edward . . 55
Hammond, John W. . 160
Harriman, Leander . 117
Harris, Nathan . . 171
Hart, Charles A. . 116
Hart, Charles B. . 116
Hawkes, Harrison F. . 214
Herrin, John . . 183
Henry, Samuel . . 117
Hill, Elisha M. . . 117
Hoban, Patrick . . 206
Hunter, Damon E. . 117
Hurd, Austin I. . . 283
Hurd, William L. . 265
Hurley, Martin V. B. . 206

I.
Ide, John S. M. . . 247

J.
Jarvis, Samuel G. . 283
Jackson, Charles R. . 172
Johnson, Levi . . 117
Judd, Charles M. . . 249
Judkins, Emery G. . 288
Judkins, George E. . 289

K.
Keller, Jacob W. . . 118
Kelley, Joseph W. . 119
Kendall, Walter B. . 80
Kenerson, George W. 172

L.
Laducer, Lewis W. . 223
Lawrence, J. Fisher . 160
Lawrence, John W. . 123
Lattimoulle, David H. 119
Levoy, Joseph . . 55
Laws, Calvin A. . 265
Lect, Eugene F. . . 55
Leet, Levi . . 206
Little, Samuel B. . . 119
Long, Charles H. . 237
Lovejoy, Russell . . 124

M.
Mace, Henry W. . . 273
Maley, James . . 125
Mann, Azro J. . . 160
Mann, Charles B. . 173
Marsh, Eli C. . . 225
Marsh, Frank E. . 125
Marston, Edwin . . 160
Marvin, Charles B. . 172
Marvin, Giles P. . . 281
Meader, Benj. L. . 266
Meader, Charles C. . 267
Merrill, Noah D. . 57
Milton, Charles A. . 56
Milton, James P. . 124
Moody, George W. . 125
Moody, William H. H. 224
Moore, Addison P. . 124
Moore, Edward F. . 224
Moore, Horatio C. . 80
Murphy, Charles H. . 173

N.
Neal, Ransom M. . . 83

Nelson, Everett W. . . 161
Nettleton, George. . . 127
Nevers, Daniel J. . . 126
Nevers, Enos B. . . 126
Nevers, Charles H. . . 126
Nevers, Frank G. . . 173
Newcomb, Albert . . 239
Nichols, Fred. A. . . 82
Nichols, David H. . . 127
Nichols, William H. . . 249
Niles, Henry H. . . 225
Noyes, Baron S. . . 125
Nutt, William H. . . 128

O.

O'Connell, Patrick . . 183
Oliver, Mitchell . . 207
Osgood, Ruel G. . . 250
Otis, Mansel . . 161

P.

Parkhurst, William C. . . 86
Parkhurst, William L. . 240
Parmalee, Albert E. . . 255
Parmalee, Charles H. . 132
Parmalee, Edward A. . . 132
Parmalee, Henry S. . . 250
Parrish, Thomas D. . . 273
Parrish, James C. . . 131
Parrish, Lyman F. . . 57
Parrish, William E. . . 131
Patrick, Henry W. . . 57
Patrick, Charles E. . . 228
Patrick, Joel W. . . 130
Paull, Henry S. . . 207
Paull, Julius B. . . 133
Pendleton, Wm. H. . . 58

Peno, Joseph . . 85
Philbrook, Charles C. . 289
Pierce, Andrew J. . . 129
Pike, Edward P. . . 130
Prentiss, John J. . . 225
Prentiss, John J., Jr. . . 132
Prentiss, Wm. Parker . 226
Putnam, Charles E. . . 58
Putnam, George H. . . 129
Putnam, John G. P. . 86

R.

Rafferty, Francis . . 240
Read, George . . 134
Read, J. Parker . . 68
Reed, Edgar T. . . 154
Reed, Levi F. . . 134
Redfield, Henry A. . . 250
Redfield, Willis . . 382
Redfield, William H. H. 282
Richardson, Joseph . . 68
Rice, William Danford 173
Roberts, John D. . . 133
Robinson, Charles D. . 133
Robinson, Otis G. . . 228
Rowell, George E. . . 186
Rowell, Henry L. . . 134
Roys, David R. . . 135
Roys, Henry F. . . 67
Rugg, John H. . . 177
Russell, Albert F. . . 256
Russell, George W. . . 177

S.

Sargent, Harvey H. . . 179
Sargent, Lyman N. . . 178
Sawyer, Samuel J. . . 228

BIOGRAPHICAL INDEX. xi

Scott, Ard	89
Scott, Charles N.	136
Scott, Henry	275
Severance, Charles L.	138
Severance, Willard C.	162
Severance, Charles E.	138
Silsbee, Henry S.	138
Sholes, Elisha S.	137
Short, Ai R.	179
Sleeper, George W.	229
Smith, Chester P.	151
Smith, Daniel B.	240
Southwick, James M.	229
Spencer, George W.	90
Sparling, Jesse	162
Sperry, Anson M.	283
Sprague, Chester M.	162
Spaulding, George W.	257
Stevens, Leonard M.	257
Still, Benjamin W.	229
Story, Charles C.	274
Story, Edward E.	154
Squier, Algernon M.	258
Stone, Cornelius H.	138
Stone, Harvey D.	240
Stowell, George H.	208
Straw, Andrew J.	69
Straw, George W.	251
Straw, John	69
Sturtevant, William S.	137

T.

Taylor, Dennis	275
Taylor, Roland	141
Tenney, George P.	70
Thorning, Samuel J.	141
Tibbels, Chester F.	142

Toothaker, Jotham S.	90
Towne, Matthew T.	141
Towne, Samuel C.	179
Tyler, Russell	155
Tyrrell, Horace A.	275
Tyrrell, Sylvanus M.	142

U.

Upham, Lorenzo M.	179

V.

Vaughan, Edwin	229
Veasey, Joel	90
Veasey, Lucius	142

W.

Walker, Andrew	162
Walker, George H.	163
Waldron, George H.	240
Wakefield, George L.	180
Wakefield, Harvey M.	143
Wakefield, Sylvester E. H.	284
Ward, Harvey	163
Waterman, George H.	269
Waterman, Harrison	269
Webb, George O.	145
Webb, Lucius C.	144
Wetherbee, Charles W.	143
Weber, George H.	91
Wheeler, John F.	70
Whitney, Horace W.	251
Whitmore, Nelson	144
Whitmore, Norman F.	90
Woodbury, Augustus E.	162

Y.

Young, Frank	145
Young, John E.	145

WAR HISTORY.

It is proposed to give a history of the part Claremont took in the War of the Rebellion. It opens with the first assault upon Fort Sumter, and closes with the assassination of Abraham Lincoln, — the last act in that great drama. It is not necessary to this history to recount the causes, running through many years, which led to the insurrection of the people of a portion of the States of the Union against the General Government, and arrayed more than a million of citizens in arms; a most bloody war, of four years' duration, involving the expenditure of almost untold treasure and the loss, on either side, of hundreds of thousands of the country's bravest and best men, carrying sorrow and mourning to many hearth-stones and multitudes of loving hearts. The causes have passed away — the effects remain to be handed down to coming generations upon the page of history; and fortunate is the man who shall make a just and impartial record of them.

While all these momentous events were transpiring, the people of Claremont had their share in them. Their coffers were opened; their young men were sent forth with a blessing—some of them to lay their lives upon the altar of their country; others to come home maimed for life, and a few to return, at the end of the great conflict of arms, weary and worn, crowned with victorious wreaths. The men raised their voices in behalf of the cause of their country, and the women gave it their unbidden tears.

On the 12th of April, 1861, South-Carolina, having a few months previously, by her legislature, passed an act seceding from the Union of States, commenced open hostilities by firing from James' Island upon Fort Sumter, garrisoned by Major Robert Anderson, and about seventy men under his command. Fort Sumter was besieged for two days, her source of supply cut off, when, on the 14th of April, Major Anderson surrendered it to the rebels, himself and his command marching out and embarking on board the United States ship Baltic, for New-York.

In his dispatch to the Secretary of War, relative to the attack and surrender of the fort, Major

Anderson says, — "Having defended Fort Sumter until our quarters were entirely burned, the main gates destroyed by fire, the gorge wall seriously injured, the magazine surrounded by flames and its door closed from the effects of heat, and three cartridges of powder only being available, and no provisions but pork remaining, I accepted the terms of evacuation offered by General Beauregard, — being the same offered by him on the 11th inst., prior to the commencement of hostilities, — and marched out of the fort on Sunday afternoon, 14th inst., with colors flying and drums beating, bringing away my company and our private property, and saluting my flag with fifty guns."

On the 15th of April President Lincoln issued a proclamation, stating that an insurrection against the government of the United States had broken out in the States of South-Carolina, Georgia, Alabama, Florida, Mississippi, Louisiana and Texas, and declared the ports of those States in a state of blockade. On the same day the President issued a call for seventy-five thousand three months volunteers, to aid in suppressing the rebellion against the Government, and called upon New-Hampshire for a regiment of militia.

On the 16th of April, in response to this call of the President, Ichabod Goodwin, then Governor of New-Hampshire, issued an order to Joseph C. Abbott, Adjutant-General, to make proclamation, calling for volunteers from the enrolled militia of the State, for one regiment of ten companies, each company to consist of three commissioned officers, four sergeants, four corporals, and sixty-four privates, with the requisite number of field and staff officers, to be uniformed, armed and equipped at the expense of the State, and to be held in readiness until called for by the United States Government.

In response to this call, Claremont was all on fire to do her share in putting down the rebellion. On the 18th of April William P. Austin enrolled his name, took the oaths prescribed, and was on that day appointed recruiting officer for the town of Claremont and vicinity. He at once opened an office for recruits and entered upon his duties. Young men flocked in faster than they could be examined and sworn.

Notice was issued for a meeting of citizens, at the town hall, on Friday evening, the 19th. At the appointed hour the building was filled to overflowing, ladies occupying the galleries. It was such a meeting of the citizens of Claremont, without distinction of party, as has seldom been held. The meeting was called to order by General Erastus Glidden, and Jonas Livingston was chosen President; Ambrose Cossit, Erastus Glidden, Walter Tufts, Thomas J. Harris, A. F. Snow, Josiah Richards and Albro Blodgett, Vice-Presidents; Edward L. Goddard and John M. Whipple, Secretaries. On taking the chair Mr. Livingston made an enthusiastic and patriotic speech. Patriotic speeches were also made by H. W. Parker, Ira Colby, Jr., A. F. Snow, Benj. P. Walker, and Samuel G. Jarvis — who deposited one hundred dollars as the nucleus of a fund for the support of the families of those who should enlist — Rev. Messrs. R. F. Lawrence and R. S. Stubbs, William P. Austin, and Henry G. Webber of Charlestown. A. F. Snow, Otis F. R. Waite, John S. Walker, Joseph Weber, Simeon Ide and George W. Blodgett, were chosen a committee to prepare and report resolutions expressive of the sentiments of the town in regard to the rebellion. The meeting was adjourned to the next evening.

On Saturday evening the town hall was again crowded, and the excitement on the increase. The exercises were opened with prayers read by Rt. Rev. Bishop Chase. The young men just enlisted by William P. Austin were marched into the hall, where front seats had been reserved for them, and met with an enthusiastic reception. As they entered the audience rose to their feet and gave them three hearty cheers. The President, Mr. Livingston, led the speaking, and was followed by Otis F. R. Waite, from the committee on resolutions, who reported the following, which were unanimously adopted:

Resolved, That all other considerations and issues are now absorbed in the one vital question, "Shall our Government be sustained?" a question of national life and independence, or of ignominious submission to the reign of barbarism and anarchy, or of unmitigated despotism!

Resolved, That the issues forced upon us by the South, and the only one presented, is the existence of any Government — and more directly of that Government under which the American people have lived and prospered for a period of eighty years.

Resolved, That for the maintenance and perpetuity of the priceless boon of civil and religious liberty, bequeathed by our forefathers in the Constitution of this Union and the free institutions it guarantees, we would imitate their example in unitedly and unreservedly tendering to the Government, if need be, "Our lives, our fortunes and our sacred honors."

Resolved, That in this first call to defend the

Constitution and the laws at the point of the bayonet, we view with patriotic pride the ready response of the noble sons of New-Hampshire and of New-England, and the Middle and Western States.

Resolved, That while our neighbors are called to defend our flag abroad, we will fill their baskets and their stores, and protect their hearth-stones at home.

Spirited and patriotic addresses were made by Charles H. Eastman, Thomas J. Harris, Arthur Chase, Simeon Ide, Thomas Kirk, Otis F. R. Waite, Rev. Carlos Marston, Heman H. Cummings, Oscar J. Brown, and Edward D. Baker, when, after three rousing cheers for the Stars and Stripes, and three more for the brave young recruits who were present, on motion of Ambrose Cossit, a committee, consisting of Ambrose Cossit, Simeon Ide and Thomas J. Harris, was appointed, to petition the selectmen to call a town meeting for the purpose of making an appropriation of two thousand dollars, or more, for the support of the families of those of our fellow-citizens who have or may enlist in defense of their country. The meeting then adjourned to the following Tuesday evening.

On Tuesday evening, the 23d of April, the people again assembled at the town hall, which was densely crowded, and many were unable to gain admittance. This seemed to be the culminating point of the excitement. General Erastus Glidden, in the absence of the President, occupied the chair. Patriotic songs were sung and fervent speeches made by John S. Walker, Chase Noyes, George W. Blodgett, William P. Austin, Henry Fitch, and Rev. R. F. Lawrence. Frank S. Fiske, of Keene, Special Aid to the Adjutant-General in the recruiting service, was present, and, being called upon, made an eloquent and stirring speech. William P. Austin was present with fifty recruits.

Immediately after the call of the President for troops, the ladies of the town bought large quantities of flannel and yarn, and went to work vigorously making shirts and drawers, and knitting socks for the soldiers. Forty or more met daily for this purpose at Fraternity Hall.

George N. Farwell and Edward L. Goddard authorized William Clark, chairman of the board of selectmen, to furnish the families of volunteers with such provisions as they might need, in his discretion, and they would hold themselves personally responsible for the same. Under these instructions families were helped to the amount of two hundred and twenty-two dollars and twenty-seven cents, which was afterward assumed by the town.

Otis F. R. Waite, of Claremont, was, on the 20th, appointed by Governor Goodwin general recruiting agent for this part of the State, to act under orders from the military head-quarters of the State. On the 29th he received the following telegram from the Adjutant-General: "Close up the stations and come on with the recruits to-morrow, as proposed. Telegraph me that you will do so. Cars will be for you at Nashua." The recruits from other stations having been sent forward, Major Waite started from Claremont, on the morning of the 30th, with eighty-five men recruited by William P. Austin. They left the village at six o'clock, and marched to the railroad station, followed by large numbers of the relatives and friends of the recruits, and other citizens. At seven o'clock, after a most touching leave-taking, which will not soon be forgotten by those who participated in or witnessed it, the company went on board the cars, which moved off amid the cheers of the three or four hundred people who had assembled to see their friends depart for the war. They went by way of Keene, Fitchburg, Groton Junction, Nashua and Manchester, arriving at Concord about three o'clock in the afternoon. At every considerable railway station multitudes of people were assembled, who gave the men their blessing and cheered them on their way.

Before leaving Claremont our citizens had provided the recruits with a full day's rations of cold meats, bread, pickles, etc.

It being understood that the recruits would have the privilege of choosing their own officers, they did so as soon as the company was full. William P. Austin was chosen Captain; John W. Lawrence, 1st Lieut.; John Dean, 2d Lieut.; Ziba L. Davis, 3d Lieut.; Homer M. Crafts, Baron S. Noyes, George H. Weber, Selden S. Chandler, Sergeants; Edward E. Story, Charles H. Parmalee, Chester F. Tibbels and Joseph Richardson, Corporals. The privates of this company were, from Claremont, Oscar C. Allen, Lyman F. Parrish, Alfred Talham, Everett W. Nelson, Edwin M. Gowdey, Ralph N. Brown, Joseph Levoy, Charles W. Wetherbee, John W. Davis, John F. Wheeler, John Straw, Wyman R. Clement, George W. Straw, Alba D. Abbott, Charles M. Judd, Heman Allen, Henry S. Morse, Albert F. Russell, Charles E. Putnam, Charles F. Colston, Edward Hall, Jerome B. Douglass, James Delmage, Charles H. Sprague, George P. Tenney, Henry W. Patrick, Joseph Peno, William H. Nichols, Ebenezer E. Cummings, Andrew J. Straw, William E. Parrish, Henry F. Roys, William H. Pendleton, Julius E. Heywood, Alanson R. Wolcott, William H. Blanchard,

Anson M. Sperry, Warren W. Howard, Dennis Taylor, Lewis W. Laducer, Albert E. Parmalee, Matthew T. Towne, J. Parker Read, Napoleon B. Osgood and Sylvester E. H. Wakefield. The other members of this company were from Acworth, Charlestown, Cornish and Unity.

A finer company of men than those enlisted by Capt. Austin has not entered the army. They enlisted from a sense of duty, the pay of privates being then but eleven dollars per month, and without the offer of bounty from town, state, or United States.

Before leaving town citizens presented the different recruits with revolvers, dirk knives, &c. At a large meeting at the town hall, on the evening of the 29th, Lieut. John W. Lawrence was presented with a sword by Sherman Livingston. The presentation speech was made by H. W. Parker, and responded to in behalf of Lieut. Lawrence by Ira Colby, Jr. George G. Ide, in behalf of the Claremont Manufacturing Company, presented each member of the company with a handsomely bound pocket Testament. The ladies gave to each two pairs of flannel drawers, two flannel shirts, woolen socks, towels, pocket-handkerchiefs, and needle-book well filled with useful articles.

On arrival at Concord the company was sent to

Camp Union; but being more than men enough already there for one regiment, they were sent to Camp Constitution, Portsmouth, where the Second Regiment was being organized. Under the call of the President for one regiment from New-Hampshire, in ten days men enough had been enlisted and sent to rendezvous at Concord and Portsmouth for more than two.

On the 3d of May the President issued a call for twenty thousand volunteers for three years, and New-Hampshire was immediately ordered to take no more volunteers for three months, but to enlist, uniform, arm, and hold, subject to orders from the War Department, a regiment of three years men. In consequence of this order the alternative was presented to the recruits then at Camp Constitution to reënlist for three years, or be discharged. Before this alternative was offered, however, the recruits were all reëxamined by a surgeon, and those found physically disqualified for service were discharged. Among these were Edwin M. Gowdey, Charles F. Colston, and Joseph F. Garfield, from Claremont.

During the organization of the Second Regiment a misunderstanding arose between Capt. Austin and one or two of the other officers, and some of the men, and the company was broken up. None of the officers chosen before the company left Claremont were commissioned. Capt. Austin and Lieut. Lawrence returned home, and Lieuts. Dean and Davis reënlisted for three years as privates. Forty-three of the men also reënlisted for three years, and were put into different companies, while the remainder were either discharged or sent to Fort Constitution, Portsmouth, to serve out the term of their enlistment.

On the 8th of May, agreeably to warrant, a town meeting was held, at which a vote was unanimously passed to appropriate a sum not exceeding twenty-five hundred dollars, to be paid to soldiers' families wherever and whenever it may be needed, and Albro Blodgett was chosen, with discretionary power, to carry out the vote. Up to March, 1862, he paid out for this purpose $2,797.23.

In most of the churches in town sermons were preached against the rebellion, and prayers offered for the success of our arms in putting it down. There was an almost unanimous expression of condemnation of the South, and political party lines seemed for a time to be almost obliterated. Every man of influence encouraged enlistments, and favored all reasonable projects for rendering aid to the families of such as had gone or might go to the war. Among the most zealous in the work of raising recruits and aiding their families, were many who, as democrats, opposed the election of Abraham Lincoln for President.

The ladies kept at work making articles needed by soldiers in hospitals and in the field; frequent meetings were held during the summer, and a most patriotic spirit was manifested among the people.

In July a company, called the Home Guard, was organized, consisting of over a hundred men—many of them past middle age, and among the best citizens of the town, all wishing to do something for the cause of the country. The company made choice of the following officers: Arthur Chase, Captain; Edwin Vaughan, 1st Lieutenant; John M. Whipple, 2d Lieutenant; Ira Colby, Jr., Francis F. Haskell, Henry S. Parmalee, William D. Rice, Sergeants; Joseph Weber, John S. M. Ide, D. C. Colby and John Geer, Corporals. The company had frequent meetings for drill, and made quite an imposing appearance.

In June, 1861, the Legislature passed an act authorizing towns to raise money by vote for the aid of families of volunteers.

About the 20th of July, Gov. Berry issued an order for enlisting, arming and equipping the Third Infantry Regiment, for three years, or during the war, and Dr. E. C. Marsh was appointed recruiting officer for Claremont and vicinity. He soon enlisted thirty-two men, and among them the following who belonged in Claremont: Frank W. Evans, David H. Grannis, Joel Veasey, Ard Scott, George W. Emerson, Alba D. Abbott, William H. Bigley, Jotham S. Toothaker, Eugene F. Leet, Horatio C. Moore, Frederick A. Nichols, Jerome B. Douglass, Norman F. Whitmore, John W. Lawrence, Joseph Peno, Charles D. Brough, John P. W. Barnard, Walter B. Kendall, George W. Spencer, Edwin M. Gowdey, William C. Parkhurst, and Albert J. Austin. These men, under the recruiting officer, left Claremont for the rendezvous of the regiment, at Concord, on the 19th day of August. The recruits attended the Methodist Church on Sunday afternoon, 18th, and Rev. Robert S. Stubbs preached a sermon, taking for his text—"Stand fast in the faith; quit you like men; be strong." On other occasions had Mr. Stubbs, through his sermons, shown forth his unconditional loyalty, and no one had doubted his entire devotion to the country; but on this occasion, when addressing men who were about to take their lives in their hands and go forth to fight for the country, he was particularly eloquent and impressive.

On the 20th of August the Governor issued an order to raise the Fourth and Fifth Regiments.

Dr. E. C. Marsh was ordered to recruit for the Fourth, and Charles H. Long was authorized to raise a company for the Fifth Regiment— the men when enlisted to choose their own company officers. All the men accepted and mustered into the service were to receive from the State a bounty of ten dollars. The men enlisted by Charles H. Long, making nearly a full company, before leaving Claremont, made choice of the following officers: Charles H. Long, Captain; Jacob W. Keller, 1st Lieutenant; Charles O. Ballou, 2d Lieutenant, who were subsequently commissioned by the Governor.

The last of September Edwin Vaughan was appointed recruiting officer, and enlisted several men who were put into different regiments then being organized.

On the 17th of February, 1862, news was received by telegraph of the capture of Fort Donelson. The bells of the village were rung, and the joy of the people manifested in other ways.

At the annual town meeting in March, 1862, it was voted that the selectmen be authorized to borrow a sum of money on the credit of the town not to exceed five thousand dollars, as it may be needed to aid the families of resident volunteers. Edward L. Goddard, Aurelius Dickinson and Alexander Gardiner were appointed a committee to designate what families were entitled to aid, and Sumner Putnam was chosen agent to pay out the money, without compensation.

On Sunday afternoon, June 22, 1862, a public meeting was held in the town hall as a demonstration of respect for the brave Claremont men who had been killed at Fair Oaks and in other battles, or died in hospitals, and of condolence with their surviving relatives and friends. A committee of arrangements had been chosen, and other preparations made at a previous meeting of citizens of the town. Otis F. R. Waite, chairman of the committee, called the meeting to order, briefly stated its objects, and presided throughout. Right Rev. Carlton Chase, Bishop of the Diocese of New-Hampshire, read selections from the Scriptures; Rev. Carlos Marston made the opening prayer; Rev. H. H. Hartwell delivered an address which had been carefully prepared, giving some account of each of those soldiers who had been killed in battle or died in hospitals, together with circumstances connected with the death of each. Short addresses were also made by Rev. Oliver Ayer, Rev. R. F. Lawrence and Rev. Mr. Marston, of Claremont, Rev. Mr. Piper of Vermont, Rev. Mr. Greeley, a native of Claremont, then settled at Methuen, Mass., Rev. Paul S. Adams, of Newport, and others.

On motion of Bishop Chase, Otis F. R. Waite was chosen historographer, to keep a record of events in Claremont which had or should transpire during the war, with a view to its being published in book form. During the meeting several appropriate pieces were sung by members of the different choirs in town. This was one of the largest and most impressive meetings held here during the war.

Early in July E. W. Woodell was appointed a recruiting officer for regiments then being formed. On the 14th, in the evening, a meeting was held for the purpose of encouraging enlistments. Walter Tufts was chosen chairman, and Joseph Weber secretary. Spirited speeches were made by D. C. Colby, Rev. Messrs. Lawrence and Marston, E. W. Woodell, George R. Lathe, and others.

Pursuant to call of the selectmen, a meeting was held on the evening of the 19th of July. Jonas Livingston was chosen chairman, and C. C. Church secretary. E. W. Woodell offered a series of resolutions re-affirming confidence in the people, the Executive of the nation, and in the army, and calling upon the people to aid in all practicable ways in raising men to fill our regiments in the field, and form new ones, as they may be needed to meet the exigencies of the country. Patriotic speeches were made by Rev. Messrs. Marston and Lawrence, E. D. Baker, C. C. Church, E. W. Woodell, and others.

On the 25th of July another meeting, with the same object in view, was held. C. H. Eastman presided. It was voted to hold a general County War Meeting, at the town hall in Claremont, on the afternoon of the 2d of the following August, and a committee appointed to make the necessary arrangements.

On the 2d of August the town hall was crowded to its utmost capacity. Henry Hubbard, of Charlestown, son of the late Gov. Henry Hubbard, presided, who, on taking the chair, made some patriotic and well-timed remarks in relation to the state of the country and the duty of loyal men. Nath'l S. Berry, Governor of the State, J. W. Patterson, Member of Congress, James W. Nesmith, U. S. Senator from Oregon, A. H. Cragin, of Lebanon, Peter Sanborn, State Treasurer, Capt. T. A. Barker, of the 2d Reg't, Major H. B. Titus, of the 9th Reg't, and other distinguished gentlemen from abroad, were present and made stirring and patriotic speeches. The hall was handsomely decorated with flags, and other emblems appropriate for the occasion. This was one of the largest and most enthusiastic meetings ever held in town.

At a legal town meeting, on the 7th of August, the following votes were unanimously passed:

Voted, That the selectmen be authorized to borrow a sum of money not exceeding five thousand dollars, to pay a bounty to citizen volunteers—the sum of fifty dollars to each—to fill the quota of three hundred thousand, when mustered into the United States service.

Voted, That the selectmen be authorized to borrow a sum of money not to exceed three thousand dollars, to pay a bounty of fifty dollars to each citizen volunteer who has or may enlist and be mustered into the U. S. service, to fill the last quota of three hundred thousand.

During the month previous to August 12, 1862, recruiting offices had been opened in town by Orville Smith, of Lempster, Sylvanus Clogston, of Washington, and E. W. Woodell, of Claremont. Up to that time they had enlisted—Mr. Smith thirty-five men; Mr. Clogston twenty-six men, and Mr. Woodell ten, a large share of whom were residents of the town. They were taken to Concord to fill old and form new regiments, as the men themselves might respectively elect.

About the middle of August William H. Chaffin was authorized to recruit men in this town for regiments then being raised in the State, and opened an office for that purpose.

At a town meeting, on the 17th of September, 1862, it was voted "to pay all resident citizens who have enlisted under the two last calls of the President, and previous to August 11, 1862, fifty dollars each when mustered into the United States service. Also, all those who have enlisted since August 11, 1862, one hundred dollars each, when mustered into the United States service," and the selectmen were authorized to borrow a sum not exceeding eight thousand dollars to carry this vote into effect.

At the annual town meeting in March, 1863, the selectmen were authorized by vote to borrow not exceeding five thousand dollars, to aid families of soldiers, — the selectmen to designate who were entitled to aid, and Sumner Putnam was chosen to pay out the money, without remuneration.

On Sunday, May 10th, a telegram was received in town announcing the capture of Richmond. It was read in the churches, bells rung, cannon fired, and other demonstrations of joy were made. It turned out that the telegram was not quite true.

The surrender of Vicksburg was celebrated in Claremont, July 7, 1863, by the ringing of bells, firing of cannon, &c. Edward F. Johnson, a son, about twenty years old, of Edwin Johnson, while assisting to fire the cannon, on Dexter Hill, was very severely injured by the premature discharge of the gun, losing the right hand and having the other badly mutilated, beside other injuries. Subsequently a considerable sum of money was contributed by citizens of the town for his benefit.

On the 5th of August, what was left of Company G, 5th Regiment, came home on a furlough. Out of eighty-one men who left town under Capt. Long, in September, 1861, less than two years before, only twelve came back. Twenty-four had been killed in battle or died of disease, and the balance had either been discharged or were left behind in hospitals. An ovation was given them at the town hall, where addresses were made by several gentlemen, and a handsome supper was provided at the Tremont House, to which about fifty citizens sat down. After the eating had been finished spirited speeches were made, sentiments offered, and the whole affair passed off very pleasantly.

On Thursday, the 6th of August, the President's Thanksgiving for the success of our arms, was observed. Business was generally suspended. Religious services were held at the Baptist Church, the Congregationalists and Methodists uniting. All three of the clergymen took part and made addresses.

On the 27th of August, 1863, the first draft in this Congressional District took place at West Lebanon. Ninety-seven men were drafted for Claremont, only four of whom, William S. Sturtevant, Jotham S. Toothaker, Charles H. Parmalee, and his brother, Edward A. Parmalee, entered the army. All the others were either rejected by the examining surgeon as unfit for duty, paid commutation, or furnished substitutes.

On the 21st of September, in town meeting, it was voted to pay drafted men, or their substitutes, three hundred dollars each, and the selectmen were instructed to borrow the money therefor.

On the 7th of December the town offered a bounty to her citizens who should enlist, of three hundred dollars, in addition to other bounties. At a previous meeting it had been voted to pay to each volunteer six hundred dollars, the town taking an assignment of the State and Government bounties.

At the annual town meeting in March, 1864, the selectmen were authorized to borrow a sum not exceeding six thousand dollars, to aid the families of volunteers and drafted men. Sumner Putnam, as agent, had paid to families of soldiers the preceding year the sum of five thousand five hundred and fifty-eight dollars and thirty-nine cents.

In May, 1864, there was another draft at the Provost Marshal's head-quarters, West Lebanon, to make up all arrearages, and thirteen men were drafted for Claremont, all of whom were exempted by the examining surgeon, or furnished substitutes. In June eight more men were drafted for the town, to make up deficiencies in her quota under all calls, none of whom entered the army.

At a town meeting, on the 23d of June, it was voted to instruct the selectmen to "pay a sum not exceeding six hundred dollars to any person who has or may hereafter enlist and be mustered into the service of the United States and counted on the quota of this town, for the present or any future call." The selectmen were also instructed to borrow a sum not exceeding six thousand dollars, for the above purpose, and also to proceed forthwith to enlist men, as opportunity may offer, in anticipation of future calls.

In August, 1864, the selectmen offered, for men to enlist into the army, bounties as follows: Two hundred dollars for one, three hundred dollars for two, and five hundred dollars for three years, beside the bounties offered by the State and United States, amounting in all, for three years men, to eleven hundred dollars.

At the annual town meeting in March, 1865, by

vote, the town treasurer was authorized to borrow a sum not exceeding seven thousand dollars to aid the families of volunteers and drafted men.

William E. Tutherly was appointed military agent to provide soldiers to fill all quotas of the town the ensuing year.

On the morning of the 14th of April, 1865, news of the taking of Richmond came by telegraph, followed on Monday morning, the 19th, by this telegram: "Official. Lee and his whole army surrendered on Sunday afternoon. Gloria!" This was soon followed by a telegram from Governor Gilmore to the selectmen, ordering them to fire one hundred guns, at the expense of the State, in honor of the overthrow of the rebellion. Business was immediately suspended, the stores closed, men, women and children were upon the streets, the church, mill and school bells were rung, and the order of the Governor was executed emphatically upon the common. Every body rejoiced at the final overthrow of the greatest rebellion on record. A meeting was notified to be held at the town hall in the evening.

At the appointed time the town hall was filled as it had seldom been filled before. The multitude was called to order by Charles M. Bingham, and Moses R. Emerson was chosen chairman, who stated the objects of the meeting and made some pertinent remarks. Rev. Edward W. Clark, pastor of the Congregational Church, opened the meeting with prayer. The congregation then united in singing, in a most thrilling manner— "Praise God from whom all blessings flow," to the tune of "Old Hundred." The Glee Club, under the direction of Francis F. Haskell, next sang a patriotic piece. Spirited addresses were made by Rev. Messrs. J. M. Peck, Edward W. Clark and E. S. Foster, Hosea W. Parker, Edward D. Baker, Ira Colby, Jr., and others. The audience arose and joined in singing "America" as it is sung only when its eloquence and beauty is fully felt by those who sing it. The meeting dissolved to witness a display of fire-works outside. Many of the public buildings and private dwellings were handsomely illuminated, and Jeff. Davis and John C. Breckenridge were burned in effigy on the Common.

On the morning of the 15th of April came a telegram announcing the assassination of President Lincoln the night before. This news turned the rejoicing of the loyal people of the North to sincere and deep mourning. On Wednesday, the 19th of April, in accordance with recommendation from Washington, and special proclamation of the Governor of New-Hampshire, the funeral obsequies of the President were observed. Business was entirely suspended; at twelve o'clock the church bells were tolled; minute guns were fired, and the people assembled at the town hall to pay their respects to the memory and worth of the murdered President, Abraham Lincoln. Never did the people of Claremont more sincerely mourn than on this occasion. Rev. Edward W. Clark read the Governor's proclamation and made the opening prayer. An appropriate piece was sung by the choir, under the direction of Francis F. Haskell. Rev. E. S. Foster read selections from Scripture; Rev. F. W. Towle offered prayer; addresses were made by Rev. Messrs. S. G. Kellogg, Moses Kimball of Ascutneyville, Vt., Foster and Towle of Claremont, Albert Goss of Auburn, N. Y., and Clark of Claremont. The choir sang the hymn commencing — "Why do we mourn departing friends," to the tune of "China," and Rev. Mr. Kimball pronounced the benediction in the most solemn manner.

FIRST REGIMENT.

This was the first regiment sent from the State to suppress the rebellion. The field officers were, Colonel, Mason W. Tappan of Bradford; Lieut. Colonel, Thomas J. Whipple of Laconia; Major, Aaron F. Stevens of Nashua. It was organized under the call of President Lincoln for seventy-five thousand three months volunteers. The men composing the first and second regiments were enlisted at the same time, and rendezvoused at Concord in April, 1861. Under this call New-Hampshire's quota was one regiment. When it was found that men enough for two regiments had been enlisted in less than ten days, it was determined to organize the first regiment at Concord, and the second at Portsmouth. The company from this town was assigned to the second regiment, and sent accordingly to the latter place.

The first regiment was organized and mustered into the United States service on the 2d of May, 1861, and left the State for Washington on the 25th of the same month. Large numbers of people assembled at the Concord railroad station to witness the departure of the regiment, and a parting salute was fired, and other demonstrations made showing the interest of the people in the event. At Manchester, Nashua, and other places on the route, the people assembled and manifested their interest in the departure of the first New-Hampshire Regiment for the seat of war. At Worcester, Mass., the citizens prepared a most bountiful entertainment for them at Mechanics' Hall. On arrival at New-York the sons of New-Hampshire resident there presented the regiment with an elegant silk banner, and gave the men an entertainment at the arsenal, and the officers a dinner at the Astor House. At Philadelphia the Soldier's Aid Society gave them a collation.

The regiment passed through Baltimore and arrived at Washington on the morning of the 28th of May, and was reviewed by President Lincoln, who complimented Col. Tappan as having the best and most thoroughly appointed regiment that had then reached the Capital. They went into camp at Kalorama, two miles from Washington, where they remained until the 10th of June, when they were brigaded with the 9th New-York and 17th Pennsylvania infantry regiments, and Capt. Magruder's Battery of Artillery, and moved to Rockville, Md., thence to Poolsville, and were engaged in guarding the Potomac, occasionally exchanging shots with the rebels. On the 5th of July the regiment marched to Point of Rocks, thence to Frederick, Winchester, Harper's Ferry, and, indeed, were kept within a radius of twenty or thirty miles, doing guard and picket duty, their marches and duties being at times arduous, and their service to the country of great importance, although they were in no pitched battles.

The regiment returned to Concord and was mustered out on the 12th of August, 1861. Many of the officers and men subsequently entered other New-Hampshire regiments and did good service. There were no men from Claremont in this regiment.

SECOND REGIMENT.

This regiment was composed mostly of men enlisted for three months, who, when the call came for three hundred thousand three years' men, reënlisted for the full term. The officers were Hon. Gilman Marston of Exeter, Colonel; Frank S. Fiske of Keene, Lieut. Colonel; and Josiah Stevens, Jr., of Concord, Major. The regiment was organized at Portsmouth.

Such of the Claremont men as were enlisted by W. P. Austin, who reënlisted for three years, were attached to this regiment, though not as a company. On account of a misunderstanding between the officers who were chosen before they left Claremont, the Company was broken up and none of them were commissioned, and the men were attached to different companies.

The regiment left Portsmouth for the seat of war, on the 20th of June, 1861. At Boston it was enthusiastically received by the Sons of New-Hampshire, reviewed by Gov. John A. Andrew, and given a handsome collation at Music Hall. At

New-York they also had a hearty reception and were presented with a beautiful stand of colors. They arrived at Washington on the 23d, and were brigaded with the First and Second Rhode-Island and Seventy-first New-York regiments, and Second Rhode-Island Battery. The brigade was commanded by Col. Ambrose E. Burnside, of the Second Rhode-Island regiment.

On the 16th of July the regiment started on its march to the disastrous field of Bull Run, with full ranks. Men who had been upon the sick-list for weeks reported for duty, fondly believing that our troops were about to strike the death-blow to the rebellion. The world knows the sanguinary character and result of this battle. Our troops were all green, and it need only be said for the Second New-Hampshire regiment that it behaved as well as any upon the field. Col. Marston was wounded in the shoulder by a rifle ball, but after having his wound dressed returned to the command of his regiment. The casualties to the regiment in this battle were seven killed, fifty-six wounded, and forty-six prisoners. Of the latter, several are supposed to have died upon the field. Andrew J. Straw, of Claremont, had his leg shot off, and is supposed to have died in the hands of the rebels.

Early in August the regiment was attached to

Brigadier-General Joseph Hooker's brigade, and passed the winter on the lower Potomac, in drilling, building corduroy roads, and the usual amusements of camp life, under different brigade commanders. On the 5th of April they embarked on steamers and joined the army in front of Yorktown. Subsequently the regiment participated in the following battles and skirmishes:

In 1862, Williamsburg, where Charles E. Putnam, of Claremont, was killed; skirmish at Fair Oaks; battle of Fair Oaks; Savage Station; Peach Orchard; Glendale; First Malvern Hill; Second Malvern Hill; Bristow Station; Second Bull Run; Chantilly; Fredericksburg. In 1863, skirmish at Manassas Gap; battles of Gettysbury; Wapping Heights. In 1864, Swift's Creek; Drury's Bluff; First Cold Harbor; Second Cold Harbor; siege of Petersburg; Fair Oaks; skirmishes at Proctor's Creek, Chesterfield, Darbytown, and Spring Hill.

The spring of 1865, when the campaign opened, found this regiment comfortably encamped at Signal Hill. On the morning of the 3d of April they broke camp and marched for Richmond, and after the evacuation of that city, occupied one of the forts overlooking its blackened ruins, for a few days. During the summer and fall they remained in Virginia, doing provost duty. They returned to Concord on the 23d of December, under command of Col. J. N. Patterson, and went into camp. On the 25th Governor Smyth gave them a handsome reception, and on the 26th the men were paid off and mustered out.

This regiment furnished many officers for other branches of the service. It was several months longer in the service than any other from this State — nearly all the men having reënlisted at the end of their first term. The men, whether officers or privates, who belonged to the Second, were careful of its reputation in the field, and are justly proud of its record.

Corporal OSCAR C. ALLEN

Enlisted under Capt. Austin, for three months, in April, and at Portsmouth for three years, and was mustered into Co. H, 2d Reg't, June 5, 1861. Appointed Corporal. He was in the battle of Williamsburg, May 5, 1862, in the battles of the Wilderness, and was soon after sent to hospital at Philadelphia, where he died of disease on the 2d of October, 1862. He came to Claremont from Woodstock, Vt., about two years before the breaking out of the rebellion; is said to have been the first man in town to enlist, and was a brave soldier.

Corporal HEMAN ALLEN

Enlisted under Capt. Austin for three months, and subsequently at Portsmouth for three years; was mustered into Co. H, 2d Reg't, June 5, 1861, and appointed Corporal. He followed the fortunes of his regiment till his muster out, June 21, 1864, when he returned home. He was one of many brave soldiers in that regiment.

SELDEN S. CHANDLER

Enlisted under Capt. Austin for three months, and subsequently at Portsmouth for three years; was mustered into Co. H, 2d Reg't, June 5, 1861, and transferred to the Fourth United States Artillery, Nov. 1, 1862.

Captain JAMES A. COOK

Was appointed Commissary-Sergeant of the 2d Regiment in June, 1861. Promoted to Quartermaster June 9, 1862. Promoted to Commissary of Subsistence, with the rank of Captain, July 2, 1863, and ordered to Point Lookout where he was Post Commissary, and had charge of provisioning from fifteen to twenty thousand prisoners, the garrison of the post and a large general hospital, from July, 1863, to May, 1864. While on what was called "Burnside's Mud March," in the winter of

1862–63, he received a severe injury in the back, from a fall, and never recovered from it. He grew worse—though all the time on duty—until May, 1864, when he was totally disabled and came home on sick leave, and in September returned to Baltimore and was discharged. While Quartermaster of the 2d Regiment he served most of the time on the Staff in one of the brigades in Gen. Hooker's division. He was a most capable, active and efficient officer, peculiarly adapted to the positions in which he was placed, always in his place and equal to any amount of work. He was born in Cornish in 1814, and died in Claremont in May, 1866, in consequence of the injury received in the army.

Sergeant HOMER M. CRAFTS

Enlisted under Capt. Austin for three months, afterward at Portsmouth for three years, and was mustered into Co. I, 2d Reg't, June 7, 1861. He was discharged for disability, May 28, 1862. Immediately after his muster he was appointed first Sergeant, which position he held until he was discharged.

WYMAN R. CLEMENT

Enlisted under Capt. Austin for three months, in April, and subsequently for three years, and was mustered into Co. H, 2d Reg't, June 5, 1861. Soon after the regiment reached Washington, young Clement was taken down with typhoid fever. When the regiment was ordered into Virginia he was left in hospital at Camp Sullivan. When his comrades returned after the disaster at Bull Run, although very sick, he inquired particularly about the battle, and showed great interest in the contest. His father, Frederick Clement, hearing of the sickness of his son, went to Washington and was with him in his last hours. He died on the 1st of August, and his remains were brought home and buried in the family lot. He was born in Woodstock, Vt., in 1839, and with his family came to Claremont in 1844, and lived here until he enlisted. The Chaplain of his regiment, Rev. Henry E. Parker, in a letter to his friends, spoke in high terms of young Clement as a faithful soldier.

JOHN DEAN

Enlisted under Capt. Austin for three months, in April, 1861, and at Portsmouth for three years. Before the company, to which he was attached, was mustered, Mr. Dean was taken down with rheumatic fever and received an honorable discharge. He enlisted again and was mustered into Co. H,

2d Reg't, Sept. 17, 1861, and was discharged for disability, March 17, 1863. Before the company enlisted in Claremont by Capt. Austin left town, the men chose their officers, and Mr. Dean was elected Second Lieutenant. The company was broken up at Portsmouth, and the men put into different companies of the 2d Regiment, as they were needed to fill up. Something of his character as a soldier may be learned from his letter giving an account of the death of his friend and fellow-soldier, Charles E. Putnam, which may be found in the notice of him. He was detailed as provost guard to Gen. Hooker's head-quarters, and was so engaged until they arrived at Harrison's Landing, July 3, 1862. During the battle of Malvern Hill the army was in three lines and the provost guard was placed in the rear to prevent straggling. Before he was aware of it, the guard to which Mr. Dean was attached had been removed, and while hunting for them he discovered a Reb. who was looking for his command, and called upon him to surrender, which he did, and was taken by Mr. Dean to head-quarters. At Harrison's Landing he was detailed to drive Gen. Heintzelman's carriage, which he did about four months, and was then appointed wagon master, and subsequently superintendent of transportation for the Department of Washington, which position he held until discharged. He is the oldest son of Horace Dean of Claremont, and is now living upon his father's farm.

Corporal ZIBA L. DAVIS

Enlisted under Capt. Austin for three months, and was chosen one of the Lieutenants of that company before it left town. On going to Portsmouth the company was broken up, none of the officers chosen were commissioned, and he reënlisted as a private for three years. He was mustered into Co. H, 2d Reg't, June 5, 1861, and appointed Corporal. He was in all the battles where his regiment was engaged until Dec. 6, 1862, when he reënlisted into Battery K, Fourth United States Artillery, and died at Falmouth, Va., January 12, 1863, of inflammation of the lungs. He enlisted April 20, 1861, and was the second man who enrolled himself in Claremont for the war. Although he was in twelve different battles and skirmishes he was never wounded; one ball, however, passed through his cap, and another through his whiskers. The Claremont boys in the 2d Regiment, on hearing of his death, immediately subscribed a sufficient sum to pay the expense, and took measures to have his body sent to his friends in Claremont. His funeral took place on the 21st, at the Methodist church, Rev. Mr. Hartwell preaching an appropriate sermon, and was very largely attended. Corporal Davis was born at Baltimore, Vt., April 12, 1839, and came to Claremont in 1856, where he learned the trade and followed the business of a house-painter. He was much respected as a citizen, and proved himself a brave and faithful soldier. He left a young widow and one boy three years old.

JOHN W. DAVIS

Enlisted under Capt. Austin for three months, afterward at Portsmouth for three years, and was mustered into Co. I, 2d Reg't, June 7, 1861. He was taken prisoner at Gettysburg, July 2, 1863, subsequently exchanged, and remained with his regiment during the term of his enlistment, at the end of which, July 21, 1864, he was discharged. He soon after enlisted in a Vermont regiment, and then into the regular army. He was once wounded in the neck. All agree that he was a brave soldier, and cheerfully performed every duty. He has not returned since the war was over.

EDWIN M. GOWDEY

Enlisted under Capt. Austin for three months, in April, 1861, went to Portsmouth where he was examined by the surgeon and discharged. In September of the same year he enlisted as a recruit and was mustered into Co. F, 2d Reg't. Discharged June 23, 1863.

EDWARD HALL

Enlisted under Capt. Austin for three months, subsequently at Portsmouth for three years, and was mustered into Co. I, 2d Reg't, June 7, 1861. He enlisted into the Second United States Cavalry, Oct. 27, 1862.

JOSEPH LAVOY

Enlisted for three months under Capt. Austin, then at Portsmouth for three years, and was mustered into Co. I, 2d Reg't, June 7, 1861. He enlisted into the Second United States Cavalry, Oct. 27, 1862.

EUGENE F. LEET

Enlisted as a recruit, and was mustered into Co. E, 2d Reg't, Sept. 17, 1861. Wounded severely in the knee at the battle of Malvern Hill, July 2, 1862. Discharged, on account of wound, at Newark, N. J., Sept. 10, 1862. Enlisted into Veteran Reserve Corps, Sept. 10, 1863. Was appointed

Drum Major in 21st Reg't Veteran Reserve Corps, Oct. 10, 1863, and served in that capacity seven months. Discharged for disability at Trenton, N. J., Aug. 9, 1865. He has never recovered from the wound received at Malvern Hill, and never can. He is a son of James Leet.

Med. Cadet CHARLES A. MILTON

Enlisted and was mustered into Co. B, 2d Reg't, June 1, 1861. Appointed Sergeant and was in the first battle of Bull Run. Appointed Medical Cadet Sept. 24, 1861, and transferred to the Medical Department U. S. Army. Died of typhoid fever at United States General Hospital, Mound City, Ill., May 15, 1862. At the time of his enlistment he was pursuing the study of medicine with Dr. Collins of Hopkinton, and had attended one course of lectures at Harvard University. His death, which occurred after a sickness of fifteen days, was deeply lamented by surgeons and attendants at the hospital where he was on duty at the time he fell sick. At a meeting for the purpose they passed resolutions of respect to Dr. Milton and of sympathy with his bereaved friends. He was born in Claremont Jan. 6, 1839, was a son of John M. Milton, and brother of James P. Milton of the 5th Reg't.

NOAH D. MERRILL

Enlisted under Capt. Austin for three months, in April, and afterward at Portsmouth for three years, and was mustered into Co. D, 2d Reg't, June 1, 1861. Died of wounds received in battle, Sept. 16, 1862. He was an orphan, and was brought up by Moses Purington of Claremont, and lived with him until twenty-one years old. Afterward, until he enlisted, he worked for different farmers in town. He was a worthy young man, and is said to have been a good soldier.

LYMAN F. PARRISH

Enlisted under Capt. Austin for three months, in April, 1861, and subsequently at Portsmouth for three years. He was mustered into Co. H, 2d Reg't, June 5, 1861. Died of disease at Manchester, N. H., Feb. 20, 1863. He was the second man in Claremont who enlisted for the war; son of the late Thomas D. Parrish of Claremont, and brother of Thomas D. Parrish of the 26th Mass. Reg't, and William E. and James C. Parrish, of Co. G, 5th Reg't.

HENRY W. PATRICK

Enlisted under Capt. Austin for three months, in April, 1861, and subsequently for three years, and was mustered into Co. H, 2d Reg't, June 5, 1861. He followed the fortunes of his regiment until he was taken down with chronic diarrhea, in November, 1862, and sent to hospital. Discharged for disability at Central Park Hospital, New-York, January 14, 1863. He is a son of William Patrick of Claremont, and brother of Joel W. Patrick of the 5th Reg't, and Charles E. Patrick of the Cavalry.

WILLIAM H. PENDLETON

Enlisted under Capt. Austin for three months, then at Portsmouth for three years, and was mustered into Co. I, 2d Reg't, June 7, 1861. Having been clerk in the post-office in Claremont for some time, he was detailed for the mail service in the army. At the expiration of his term of enlistment, June 21, 1864, he was mustered out.

CHARLES E. PUTNAM

Enlisted under Capt. Austin for three months, in April, 1861, and subsequently for three years, and was mustered into Co. H, 2d Reg't, June 5, 1861. He was in the first Bull Run battle, July 21, and, in a letter to his brother George, who was then at home, but afterward enlisted in the 5th

Reg't, and was killed at Cold Harbor, under date of July 26, 1861, thus speaks of that great disaster:

"*Dear Brother:*—Your letter was handed to me after we were formed in line to march, last Saturday morning, and I read it as we stopped to rest. I was very glad to hear from you, and that the folks at home were all well. I tell you what it is, George, that was the hardest day's work I ever did. We started at 2 o'clock in the morning, marched eighteen miles, and right on to the battle-field, without any rest or breakfast, and many of the men had no water in their canteens. We were stationed on a hill at the right of the Rhode-Island Battery, to support it, and where the enemy could pour their shot and shell right into us, and they came thick and fast. Poor Eastman, who had marched the first in my rear all day, was the first man shot.

"I wish I could give you a description of the field and battle, but have not time nor room. Men never fought more bravely than did the Federal troops on that day. It was an awful sight to see such brave men slaughtered as they were, and what looked almost as bad, to see the noble horses cut to pieces by the cannon balls. Griffin's Battery that went on to the field in the morning with one hundred and sixty-nine noble horses, and all were killed but two; one of these was the Captain's, and the other one of the cannoneers cut loose and rode into Washington. This was all there was left of one of the best batteries in the United States. Ellsworth's Zouaves were there and fought like fiends. As they charged upon the enemy they would shout Ellsworth, and rush on, and well did they avenge him that day.

We fought them nine hours, and looked in vain for reënforcements. Many were out of ammunition, and we were compelled to retreat. When the order was given I was assisting in carrying off a man that was sun-struck, and did not leave the field until our regiment had got almost a mile the start of me. I then started and went more than half a mile under a galling fire from the enemy. Sometimes the cannon balls struck so near that they would throw the dirt all over me, but I kept on until I got to the hospital, where I stopped a few moments to see some of our wounded. It was in an old stone church. I went in and looked through it, and I pray God that I may never witness another such a sight. I left and came on about ten rods, and found two of our own company that were wounded. One was Jack Straw. He had his leg shot off below the thigh—wanted water — got them some and started on. I found I was behind my regiment. Saw our cavalry stationed on a hill to cover our retreat, and started for them. When I got within thirty or forty rods of them a party of the enemy's black horse cavalry came out of the woods and gave us a volley from their rifles. The balls whistled about my ears, but I kept on and overtook the main body, and came into Washington safe and sound, but with the sorest feet I ever had. I was obliged to pull my boots off and walk in my stocking feet. During thirty-six hours we marched over sixty miles, beside being on the field seven hours, with nothing to eat but hard bread, and nothing to drink but muddy water.

"We had four men killed in our company, nine wounded, and five missing. I am entirely well now. They say we must try them again next week. I am ready to go, and if I fall I know I shall be avenged. I know it is a just cause, and am willing to go where duty calls."

Mr. Putnam was killed at the battle of Williamsburg, Va., on the 5th of May, 1862. Under date of May 11th, 1862, his Captain, Littlefield, wrote to his father, and after telling him of the death of his son, says — "Sad as this intelligence must be to you, you have the consolation of knowing that he was a noble man. He was honest and faithful in the discharge of all his duties; ever ready and always in his place; kind alike to his officers and comrades, and was loved and esteemed by every member of my company. His kindness to me, and his manly bearing, had taught me to love him like a brother. He fell while manfully fighting for his country." He was buried by his comrades near the battle ground, and his name marked on a tree at his head. He was twenty-seven years old, and left to mourn his loss a father, Zelotes Putnam, —since dead—a mother, one sister, two brothers, one of whom, George, was killed at Cold Harbor, Va., June 3, 1864, and many friends.

The following is a portion of a letter from John Dean, son of Horace Dean of this town, to his mother, dated Williamsburg, Va., May 8, 1862. It is of such a character as to be worth a place in this history. There may be more interesting accounts of the battle of Williamsburg, but none more so to the people of Claremont than that contained in this letter, as it connects our noble 2d Regiment and our brave Claremont men with one of the most sanguinary battles of the war:

"On Sunday morning, May 4th, we discovered for a certainty that the enemy had evacuated Yorktown, and at noon we were ordered to advance in pursuit. We marched as fast as our legs would carry us until half past ten at night, then laid down just as we were, with our guns by our side. About two in the morning it commenced raining very hard, and at four we started on. The mud was awful, and we had to wade right through it. In a very few moments, our clothes and blankets being wet, and our feet and legs covered with mud, it was with difficulty we could get along. About six o'clock our advance guard were fired on by the enemy's rear, just as they emerged from a piece of wood into a piece of felled timber. The 1st Massachusetts regiment were in advance, the 2d New-Hampshire next. The Massachusetts regiment formed into line of battle and advanced on the left — our regiment in front. As soon as we started out of the woods the enemy opened a battery directly in front of us; and just as we crossed the road a cannon ball, the first one fired, went right through our ranks, killing one and wounding two of our company. Then commenced a shower of balls, and we were ordered to keep under cover as much as possible — the fallen trees affording us a good protection. We advanced from one tree to another about fifty rods, to the edge of a large open field in front of the enemy's breastworks. They were pouring a deadly fire into us, and Gen.

Hooker ordered one of our batteries up in front of us to engage their battery, but before they got their guns in position all but three of the men belonging to the battery were killed, and one of their guns stuck in the mud. For a few moments the guns were left entirely alone! Oh, if you could have seen the Captain, his hat off, crying, as he turned round and shouted, "For God's sake send me some men to work these guns!" The rebels, seeing the guns deserted, came out of their intrenchments and were about to make a charge to capture them; but immediately the boys of our regiment, without any order, fixed bayonets and rushed out to receive them, when they ran back into their intrenchments. About a hundred of us then caught hold of the gun that was stuck in the mud and took it into position in an instant. By this time some men arrived to work the guns, ammunition began to arrive, and until about noon it was fight in earnest. Our battery had to contend with two — one in front, and one on the left — we lying all the time within eight rods of the enemy's guns! The rebel sharp-shooters by noon had killed nearly all the gunners, and the guns were all disabled but one, the horses all dead, and the cannon and musket balls showering around us. We were ordered to fall back. Charles Putnam and myself, who had been lying together behind a log, were just eating some hard bread and molasses, several balls and shells having hit within a few inches of us—one ball grazing the leg of my pants. We started with our Captain, but it was impossible to keep the company together, as the surroundings presented a perfect slash of heavy timber. Charles and myself, however, agreed, if the company did not get formed, to remain together.

We fell back, amid a perfect shower of balls, to the edge of the woods where we started from. We there held a consultation as to what we should do. It looked as if the day was going against us, and we agreed to lay off our knapsacks and overcoats, loaded our guns anew, for fear they would not go, as it was raining hard all the time. "Now," said Charles, "as we can't find the regiment, let us go where there is the most fighting, and sell ourselves as dearly as possible!" I told him I would agree to it. We then shook hands, and each told the other what he had in his pockets, what one was to do if the other should fall, and started.

At this time, about 2 o'clock P. M., the New-Jersey brigade, belonging to our division, were having a struggle with a large force who were trying to flank us on the left. I saw Major Stevens, and asked him where we could do the most good. He replied, "Up with the Jerseys," and that he was trying to get the regiment together and send them there. We then started on a run and came up with the "Jerseys" within fifty rods of a large force of rebels. We then commenced loading and firing, taking good aim every time. Part of the time the rebels would fall back slowly, and then, being reinforced, would force us back, we continuing to load and fire behind each tree as we advanced or retreated, until we had used all our cartridges but two or three. Charles and myself were behind a large pine tree. I was in the act of driving a ball into my gun — he had just fired, got his gun reloaded and started for another tree, a little further ahead — when I happened to look that way just in time to see him pitch forward, his face down! Oh, my God! what were my feelings at that moment! I was immediately at his side, turned him over, and found that he was shot through the brain. The ball passed through the front piece of his cap, entering the head just above the left eye, and coming out exactly opposite on the back side of the head. I took his pocket-book and purse, containing together ten dollars and forty-five cents, with a few other articles. His knapsack, as well as my own, was lost. A hunt for them would be useless, as the battle-field was soon stripped of every thing worth carrying away.

"Joseph Richardson, Oscar Allen, John Straw, Henry Patrick,—all from Claremont—and myself went and buried him on the bank of a small stream. A pine tree marks the head of his grave, and a small beech tree stands at his feet, upon both of which we cut his name and the letter of his company. Poor fellow! Not a man in his company but feels sad, and not an hour passes but I hear some one say, "Poor Charles! It is a pity such a brave fellow should fall!" A braver fellow never lived. He had endeared himself to his comrades, as well as to his officers, and his example is worthy of imitation."

Rev. Mr. Hartwell preached his funeral sermon, at the Methodist church, on Sunday, the 18th of May, which was very largely attended.

HENRY F. ROYS

Enlisted under Capt. Austin for three months, and at Portsmouth reënlisted for three years; was mustered into Co. H, 2d Reg't, June 5, 1861, served faithfully and bravely the term of his enlistment, and was mustered out June 21, 1864.

Sergeant JOSEPH RICHARDSON

Enlisted under Capt. Austin for three months, and subsequently at Portsmouth for three years. He was mustered into Co. H, 2d Reg't, June 5, 1861; appointed Corporal Nov. 1, 1862; promoted to Sergeant Feb. 1, 1864; was in all the battles in which his regiment was engaged, behaving with great coolness and bravery, and was mustered out at the end of his term of enlistment, June 21, 1864.

J. PARKER READ

Enlisted for three months under Capt. Austin, then at Portsmouth for three years, and was mustered into Co. I, June 7, 1861. At the time of his enlistment he was less than seventeen years old. He was in the two Bull Run battles, at Williamsburg, the Wilderness, seven days, and indeed all the battles where his regiment was engaged, until the first of November, 1862, when he was placed in hospital on account of distressing chronic diarrhea. He was honorably discharged at Central Park Hospital, New-York, Dec. 23, 1862, and returned home, but it was many months before he recovered. He was the youngest son of the late Jonathan Read, and brother of George Read of the Fifth Regiment, who died of chronic diarrhea in hospital at Newark, N. J.

ANDREW J. STRAW

Enlisted under Capt. Austin for three months, in April, and subsequently for three years, and was mustered into Co. H, 2d Reg't, June 5, 1861. He was mortally wounded in the battle of Bull Run, July 21, 1861, fell into the hands of the enemy, and is supposed to have died soon after. The last heard of him is the account of Charles E. Putnam, in his letter to his brother George, which is given in full in the notice of his death. Straw is believed to have been the first Claremont man who gave his life for his country in the war of the rebellion. He was a son of the late Daniel J. Straw of Claremont, brother of John Straw, of the same company, and George W. Straw of the Sharp-shooters.

JOHN STRAW

Enlisted under Captain Austin for three months, in April, and subsequently at Portsmouth for three years, and was mustered into Co. H, 2d Reg't, June 5, 1861. Wounded in the calf of the leg at the first battle of Bull Run, July 21, 1861. Wounded in the foot by a minnie ball, and also in the back by a piece of shell, at the battle of Williamsburg, May 5, 1862. Discharged for disability Feb. 1, 1863. Enlisted and was mustered into Co. A, Heavy Artillery, May 26, 1863; served to the end of the war and was mustered out with his company Sept. 11, 1865. He died in the summer of 1867. He was a son of the late Daniel J. Straw of Claremont, and brother of Andrew J. Straw of the same company, who was killed at the first battle of Bull Run, and George H. Straw of the Sharp-shooters.

Sergeant GEORGE P. TENNEY

Enlisted under Capt. Austin for three months; went to Portsmouth and reënlisted for three years; was mustered into Co. H, 2d Reg't, June 5, 1861; appointed corporal and promoted sergeant Sept. 1, 1861. Was in most of the battles with the regiment until his term of enlistment expired, and was mustered out June 21, 1864. He was a true soldier and is a good man. He is the youngest son of the late Amos J. Tenney of Claremont, and is now in business at Lyndon, Vt.

JOHN F. WHEELER

Enlisted under Capt. Austin for three months, in April, and afterwards at Portsmouth for three years, and was mustered into Co. A, 2d Reg't, May 31, 1861. He was in the first Bull Run battle, taken prisoner and sent to Richmond, where he remained about three months, when with others he was sent to New-Orleans, where he was kept until the 6th of February, 1862, when he, with others, was started on foot for Salisbury, N. C., and arrived there on the 15th, where he remained until June, when he was exchanged, and died on shipboard between Salisbury and New-York, June 8, 1862, of dysentery. His remains were sent to his friends at Cambridge, Vt., where his father, Rev. Lovell Wheeler, resides. He had been in the employ of Messrs. Brown & Hart, of Claremont, about two years before the breaking out of the rebellion.

THIRD REGIMENT.

This was the second regiment raised in this State under the President's call for three years men. It was recruited throughout the State, though Manchester furnished three companies. The Field officers were Enoch Q. Fellows of Sandwich, Col.; John H. Jackson of Portsmouth, Lieut. Colonel; John Bedel of Bath, Major. Col. Fellows was a graduate of West Point, and Lieut. Col. Jackson and Major Bedel had served in the Mexican War. The regiment was recruited the first part of August, 1861, mustered into the United States service on the 25th, and was assigned to a corps being formed for a secret service by Gen. W. T. Sherman. The State paid to each man mustered into this regiment a bounty of ten dollars.

The regiment broke camp at Concord on the 3d of September, and embarked for Hampton Plains, Long Island, twenty-five miles from New-York, the rendezvous of the expedition. On the 14th the regiment was ordered to Washington, D. C., and went into camp, and on the 19th of October embarked on board a steamer for Fortress Monroe, under command of Gen. Sherman; from thence to Port Royal, arriving there on the 4th of November. Col. Fellows resigned on the 12th of June, 1862.

The following is a list of the battles, sieges, reconnoissances and skirmishes in which the regiment was engaged: Port Royal Harbor, S. C., November 7, 1861; Elba Island, Ga.; Bluffton, S. C.; Jehossee, S. C.; James Island, S. C. [Horatio C. Moore and Joseph Peno of Claremont, were killed in this battle.] Secessionville, S. C.; Pocotaligo, S. C., in 1862; May River, Fla.; Stono Inlet, S. C.; Morris Island, S. C.; Fort Wagner, S. C.; Siege of Wagner; Siege of Sumter, from Sept. 7, 1863, to March 1, 1864; Pilatka, Fla.; Chester Station, Va.; Drury's Bluff, Va.; Bermuda Hundred, Va.; Wier Bottom Church, Va.; Petersburg, Va.; Hatcher's Run, Va.; Flussel's Mills, Deep Bottom, Va.; Siege of Petersburg from August 24 to September 29; Newmarket Heights, Va.; Demonstration on Richmond, Sept. 29, and Oct. 1, 1864; Newmarket Road, Va.; Darbytown Road, Va.; Charles City Road, Va.; Fort Fisher, N. C., Jan. 15, 1865; Sugar Loaf Hill, N. C.; Smith's Creek and N. E. Station, N. C.

The Third was one of the best regiments that went from New-Hampshire, doing its full share of fighting and campaigning, and suffering great losses of officers and men in battle and from disease incident to exposure in the field.

On the 20th of July, 1865, the regiment was mustered out of the United States service and ordered to New-Hampshire. It arrived at Concord on the 28th, with twenty-six officers and three hundred and twenty-four men. They had a warm reception from the Governor, and the men were finally discharged on the 3d of August.

ALBERT J. AUSTIN

Enlisted and was mustered into Co. F, 3d Reg't, August 23, 1861. Reënlisted Feb. 13, 1864. Appointed company clerk in July, 1862. Wounded at the battle of Deep Run, August 16, 1864. Promoted to Corporal May 1, 1865. In September, 1864, he was detailed as attendant on board hospital steamer George Leary, where he remained until the following December, when he resumed his old duties as company clerk. In March, 1865, he was detailed as Clerk in the Provost Marshal's office at Wilmington, N. C., and the following May as chief clerk in the Provost Marshal's office at Goldsborough, N. C., which position he held until the regiment started for home, in July. He was very efficient and faithful in whatever position he was placed. After the war was over he came home and resumed his former business as a file manufacturer.

ALBA D. ABBOTT

Enlisted first under Capt. Austin, in April, 1861, for three months, went to Portsmouth, and declining to enlist for three years was discharged and returned home. He enlisted again and was mustered into Co. A, 3d Reg't, Aug. 22, 1861, served faithfully, and reënlisted Feb. 12, 1864; was mustered out with his regiment and returned home.

DANIEL S. ALEXANDER

Enlisted as a recruit, and was mustered into Co. F, 3d Reg't, Sept. 19, 1862. He was killed at the battle of Drury's Bluff, Va., May 13, 1864. Was a farmer by occupation, and step-son of the late Capt. Matthew Porter, formerly of Claremont.

JOHN P. W. BARNARD

Enlisted and was mustered into Co. F, 3d Reg't, August 23, 1861. He was discharged July 28, 1862.

Sergeant WILLIAM H. BIGLEY

Enlisted and was mustered into Co. A, 3d Reg't, Aug. 22, 1861. He was appointed Corporal and promoted to Sergeant Aug. 5, 1863. Reënlisted Feb. 27, 1864. He followed the fortunes of his regiment from first to last, was mustered out after the war was over, and returned home. He enlisted from a high sense of duty to his country, and did it to the utmost of his ability.

CHARLES CARROLL

Enlisted as a recruit and was mustered into Co. D, 3d Reg't, Aug. 29, 1862. Mustered out June 26, 1865.

SANFORD COLBURN

Enlisted as a recruit, and was mustered into Co. H, 3d Reg't, Sept. 19, 1862. Wounded severely in the arm at the battle of Morris Island, July, 1863. Transferred to the Veteran Reserve Corps, May 31, 1864.

Corporal ALBERT G. DANE

Enlisted and was mustered into Co. A, 3d Reg't, August 23, 1861. Appointed Corporal. Reënlisted February 12, 1864. Wounded slightly July 10, 1863. Taken prisoner at Laurel Hill, Va., Oct. 7, 1864, and died at Salisbury, N. C., Feb. 3, 1865. His sufferings and experience in prison were not unlike those of John G. P. Putnam, of the same regiment, except that his constitution broke down under it, while Putnam alone, of the four from his regiment who were in Salisbury prison, lives to tell the story of his own and their treatment at the hands of their rebel captors. He was a son of the late John Dane of Claremont, and was a good soldier.

JEROME B. DOUGLASS

Enlisted and was mustered into Co. F, 3d Reg't, August 23, 1861. Discharged for disability at DeCamp Hospital, June 23, 1864.

GEORGE W. EMERSON

Enlisted and was mustered into Co. F, 3d Reg't, Aug. 23, 1861. He served the full term of his enlistment, and was mustered out Aug. 23, 1864.

Corporal FRANK W. EVANS

Enlisted and was mustered into Co. A, 3d Reg't, Aug. 22, 1861. He was appointed Corporal; was in the battle at Morris Island, S. C., July 10, 1863, where he lost an arm, on account of which he was discharged Nov. 10, 1863, and came home. He is a son of Rev. W. F. Evans. No one ever questioned his bravery as a soldier, or his integrity as a man. He is but one of many who have given a limb to their country.

DAVID H. GRANNIS

Enlisted and was mustered into Co. A, 3d Reg't, Aug. 22, 1861. Was in the battle of James Island, June 16, 1862, and had his canteen shot away, but was not injured. Died of diphtheria in hospital at Hilton Head, March 4, 1863. He first enlisted in a Vermont three months regiment; while in camp and when the regiment left the State, was sick with measles so he could not go with them and was discharged. Was twenty-seven years old when he died; was a son of the late Col. David and Olive S. Grannis of Claremont, and half brother of Edward E. Story of the 6th Reg't, and Charles C. Story of the 6th Massachusetts Reg't. Mr. Grannis was a house painter by trade, and a worthy, upright young man.

JOHN GILBERT

Enlisted and was mustered into Co. F, 3d Reg't, Aug. 23, 1861. Served faithfully, being in all the actions and skirmishes in which his regiment participated, until Aug. 16, 1864—seven days before his term of service expired—when he was killed in the battle of Deep Run, Aug. 16, 1864. He was left upon the field, and his body fell into the hands of the enemy. He was a most brave and faithful soldier, and left a wife and three children living in Cornish.

Corporal TRACY L. HALL

Enlisted as a recruit, and was mustered into Co. H, 3d Reg't, Sept. 22, 1862; promoted to Corporal Nov. 25, 1863; wounded June 16, 1864; mustered out with his regiment, June 26, 1865. He was a faithful soldier.

Corporal WALTER B. KENDALL

Enlisted and was mustered into Co. F, 3d Reg't, Aug. 23, 1861. Promoted to Corporal. Reënlisted Feb. 21, 1864. Killed in front of Petersburg, June 16, 1864. He left a young wife, and is said to have been a brave soldier.

Sergeant HORATIO C. MOORE

First enlisted and was mustered into the Massachusetts 3d Regiment for three months, in April, 1861. He served the full term of his enlistment in that regiment, and when it was mustered out returned to his home in Claremont, in August. Very soon after his return he enlisted for three years under E. C. Marsh, went to Concord alone and in advance of the other men, went into camp with the 3d Regiment, then being formed there, and when the regiment was mustered was appointed second Sergeant of Co. F, on the 23d of

August, 1861. In the engagement at James Island, near Charleston, S. C., on the 16th of June, 1862, he was mortally wounded by a minnie ball, which entered his right cheek and lodged in the neck. He never spoke after he was wounded, but was in full possession of his senses to the last moment of his life. He was carried from the field to camp, where he remained two days, when he was sent, with other wounded of his regiment, to the hospital at Hilton Head, under the care of George W. Emerson and George W. Spencer of Claremont, but died on the passage and was buried in a lot prepared by his company, the fall before, at Hilton Head. He was twenty-three years old, and gave his noble young life to his country. His Captain, J. F. Randlett, in a letter to his father, speaking of his death, wrote: "He was a faithful man in the position he held, and would no doubt have risen had his valuable life been spared. With a cheerful disposition and temperate habits he made for himself friends with all with whom he was associated, and a gloom rests upon our hearts, at mention of his sad fate, that time will never remove. About four weeks before his death I had a conversation with him, and spoke of his prospects and of what a few months would do. His reply was, 'Captain, I shall be dead before that time.' "

Young Moore was a printer by profession, having served his time in the National Eagle office with the writer hereof, and was a member of his family four years, from May, 1854, to May, 1858, and seemed almost like a son and brother. He was intelligent, faithful and honest as an apprentice, and polite, kind and affectionate as a member of the family. When he left the Eagle office he went to Keene, and afterwards worked at Nashua and Concord, this State, Bridgeton, Me., and West Brookfield, Boston and Cambridge, Mass., and was at the latter place when he enlisted. He was one of the very first men to respond to the call of the President for seventy-five thousand volunteers for three months. He was a son of Curtis Moore of Claremont, and a brother of Addison P. Moore of the 5th Regiment. His funeral sermon was preached in the Baptist church, in July, by Rev. Mr. Ayer. In December following his death, through the kind offices of Capt. J. F. Randlett, his body was sent home, and buried in the family lot with appropriate ceremonies at the grave.

Corporal FREDERICK A. NICHOLS

Enlisted and was mustered into Co. F, 3d Reg't, Aug. 23, 1861. He reënlisted Feb. 21, 1864, and was appointed Corporal; was in most of the battles in which his regiment participated, until the skirmish in which he received his fatal wound, near Bermuda Hundred, June 16, 1864. A minnie ball entered at the shoulder and passed down into the body so that the surgeon was unable to find it. He was carried to the regimental hospital, where he died the next morning, and was buried by his company, the chaplain of the regiment performing service. He was born at Lynn, Mass., Aug. 30, 1841, and a half brother of William H. Nichols of Co. E, Sharp-shooters. When he was at home on his veteran furlough he was married, March 27, 1864, to Ellen, daughter of Abial White of Claremont. His captain, in a letter to his wife, giving the particulars of his death, wrote:

"He was a good and brave soldier, and died at his post while bravely defending his country and his country's flag from the foul hands of traitors. He was always ready and willing to do his duty, and was to be found at his post in the hour of danger. His loss is deeply felt by the company, and they all, as well as myself, sympathize with you in your sad bereavement."

RANSOM MERRITT NEAL

Enlisted as a recruit, and was mustered into Co. A, 3d Reg't, Aug. 30, 1862. He died in camp at

Hilton Head, S. C., on the 30th of October, of the same year, of diphtheria, caused by exposure while on duty. At the time of enlisting, his health was not firm, but he wished to do what he could for his country in her time of need. A letter from the Captain of his company, R. F. Clark, to Mr. Neal's young wife, says, "He joined my company on his arrival here, some weeks ago. He was faithful in the performance of his duties; a sympathizing friend in time of need; quiet in his daily pursuits; intelligent and well-informed, he won the love and respect of all who knew him before the battle-field had tried his courage. On the 21st we were ordered on an expedition to Pocotaligo, where it was supposed we should meet the enemy. Your husband was advised to remain in camp, and not accompany us, his appearance seeming to indicate that he could not stand the fatigue and exposure of the march. He refused to remain behind, although my permission to have had him would have been freely given. He went with us, and there also he was faithful to his trust and foremost among the men in doing his duty. The march, with the exposure and fatigue, without doubt hastened his end. While you have lost a husband, I have lost a noble soldier, and many have lost a dear friend. He is to be buried at 2 o'clock this P. M." He kept a daily journal, and just before this expedition he wrote in it, "If I go, and fall, I shall only regret that I have not been able to do more for my country than to lay down one poor life." Mr. Neal was a printer by trade, having served his time in the Northern Advocate office, and had contributed many articles, both prose and verse, of some merit for one of his age, to the press. He was a member of the Methodist Episcopal Church, and a young man of probity and worth. For some time before his death he had felt it to be his duty to fit himself for the ministry, and was doing so at the time he enlisted. He was the only son of Lewis Neal, formerly of Unity, but for the last few years a resident of Claremont village. At the time of his death he was twenty-four years old, and left a young wife. His funeral services were attended at the Methodist Church, on Sunday, Nov. 23, 1862, and an appropriate sermon preached by Rev. Mr. Hartwell.

JOSEPH PENO

Enlisted under Capt. Austin in April 1861, for three months, and was sent to Fort Constitution to serve out his term of enlistment. Enlisted again and was mustered into Co. C, 3d Reg't, Aug. 23, 1861. Killed in the battle of James Island, S. C., June 16, 1862, and was buried by his fellow-soldiers.

WILLIAM C. PARKHURST

Enlisted and was mustered into Co. F, 3d Reg't, Aug. 23, 1861, and was discharged September 23, 1861. He afterward enlisted in a New-York regiment. He was not a native of Claremont, and but little is known of his subsequent history.

JOHN G. P. PUTNAM

Enlisted as a recruit, mustered into Co. A, 3d Reg't, Sept. 19, 1862; taken prisoner at Deep Bottom, with about five hundred others, August 16, 1864. The next day they were all taken to Libby Prison, Richmond, where they were stripped, searched and relieved of all valuables, and kept three days without any kind of food. Then they were given a piece of corn bread two inches square and half a pint of bean soup, which they ate with a relish. From there they were taken on the 21st to Belle Isle, where they had no shelter to cover them, and had for food a piece of corn bread about two inches square and not more than two ounces of tolerable bacon in the morning, and in the afternoon a piece of bread of like size and quality and what they called half a pint of bean soup. Two Shaker pailfuls of this soup was allowed for each hundred men, and often this quantity of soup would not contain more than a quart of beans.

The beans were cooked in the water in which the meat was boiled that they had in the morning. The top of the soup would be almost covered with bean bugs — an article little known in New-England — and maggots. The ground where seven thousand men were confined was about two hundred and thirty by two hundred and thirty-five yards square. After a few days some old tents — enough for about two thirds of the prisoners — were given them, but they had no straw or blankets to lie upon. In this situation and with this food they were kept until the 4th of October, when they were given four days' rations and started for Salisbury, N. C., arriving there on the 6th, and were placed in the well known Salisbury prison, where they remained until February 22d, 1865, when they were sent to Wilmington, paroled on the 2d of March, and sent to Annapolis, Md., where they found comfortable food and quarters. Of the ten thousand prisoners at Salisbury when Putnam was there, but four thousand lived to be paroled. Among those who died during the time were Ard Scott and Albert G. Dane of Claremont, and George W. Constantine of Charlestown.— Scott died November 20, 1864, Constantine on the 27th of January, and Dane on the 3d of February, 1865. When they first went to Salisbury each man was given for a day's rations a pound of bread, and in the morning a gill of molasses, or a small piece of meat, and in the afternoon a half pint of rice soup. As the number of prisoners increased the rations grew proportionately less. At some times they subsisted for five days on a pint of cob-meal each. Until the middle of November they had no shelter; after which they had tents for a part, while others dug for themselves holes in the ground. When Putnam was taken prisoner he weighed one hundred and forty-four pounds, and when he was paroled he weighed less than a hundred, and was so blind, from weakness, that he could not see to distinguish one man from another at ten paces distant. He was discharged and came home in June, 1865. In October, 1867, he appeared before the Congressional Commission in session in Boston, and testified in relation to his experience in rebel prisons. Mr. Putnam is a native of Italy, came to this country when twelve years old, and was twenty-three when he enlisted. He now lives in Claremont, and has told his own story, not one quarter of the horrors of which is given here. His experience is that of tens of thousands of other brave and noble young men who suffered more than a hundred deaths for the country.

Sergeant ARD SCOTT

Enlisted and was mustered into Co. F, 3d Reg't, Aug. 23, 1861; promoted to Corporal Dec. 1, 1861. Reënlisted for a second term of three years or during the war, Feb. 21, 1864; promoted to Sergeant, and soon to first Sergeant. He was taken prisoner Oct. 1, 1864, at Darbytown, Va., carried to Richmond, thence to Belle Isle, and thence sent to Salisbury, N. C., and was there with John G. P. Putnam, Albert G. Dane and Samuel W. Chapman of Claremont, and George W. Constantine of Charlestown, and died of starvation and exposure on the 20th of November, 1864. His experience while in prison is not unlike that of Putnam, which is given more fully in the notice of him. He kept a diary in which he made daily entries up to the 13th of November, after which he was too feeble in body and mind to take cognizance of what was going on around him. The diary was taken by his brother-in-law, Chapman, and returned to Sergeant Scott's mother. This record will forever stand to show the torture and worse than murder committed upon our men at Salisbury prison. Sergeant Scott was a son of the late Horace H. Scott of Claremont, and was a brave and faithful soldier.

GEORGE W. SPENCER

Enlisted as a musician, and was mustered into Co. K, 3d Reg't, Aug. 24, 1861; served faithfully the full term of his enlistment, and was mustered out Aug. 23, 1864. He is a printer by trade, having served an apprenticeship in the National Eagle office, and resumed his profession when he returned from the army.

JOTHAM S. TOOTHAKER

Enlisted and was mustered into Co. F, 3d Reg't, Aug. 23, 1861. Discharged for disability Dec. 13, 1862. Drafted at West Lebanon, Aug. 27, 1863, and mustered into Co. E, 5th Reg't, Oct. 14, 1863. Wounded June 17, 1864, and was mustered out with that regiment June 28, 1865.

JOEL VEASEY

Enlisted as a musician and was mustered into Co. F, 3d Reg't, Aug. 23, 1861. At the end of his term of enlistment he was mustered out, Aug. 23, 1864, and returned home. He is a brother of Lucius Veasey of the 5th Regiment.

Corporal NORMAN F. WHITMORE

Enlisted and was mustered into Co. A, 3d Reg't, Aug. 22, 1861. Promoted to Corporal. Transferred to the United States Signal Corps, Sept. 7, 1863. He was wounded severely, July 10, 1863, in the siege of Fort Wagner, losing his right eye. He never fully recovered from his wounds, although he was much of the time on duty until April, 1864, when he went into hospital at Jacksonville, Fla., and died of disease occasioned by his wounds, June 9, 1864, and was buried by his comrades. He enlisted very soon after finishing a course and graduating at Kimball Union Academy, Meriden, and was a son of Elijah Whitmore of Claremont. His funeral sermon was preached by Rev. Mr. Ayer, at the Baptist church, on Sunday, June 26. He was a worthy, upright, intelligent young man.

GEORGE H. WEBER

Enlisted under Capt. Austin, in April, 1861, for three months, went to Portsmouth, and declining to reënlist for three years, was discharged. He enlisted again and was mustered into Co. K, 3d Reg't, Aug. 24, 1861. Discharged for disability July 29, 1862. He enlisted again and was mustered into Co. D, 8th Reg't, Sept. 2, 1862; was wounded at the storming of Port Hudson, May 27, 1863, and was discharged, on account of wounds, at New-Orleans, Sept. 2, 1863. He is a son of Joseph Weber, Esq., editor of the Northern Advocate, and a printer by trade. During a portion of the time that he was in the army he was detailed to work in different printing offices. He is now at work at his trade in Boston.

FOURTH REGIMENT.

This regiment was organized at Manchester, the State giving to each man on being mustered into service, a bounty of ten dollars. The Field officers were Thomas J. Whipple of Laconia, Colonel; Louis Bell of Farmington, Lieut. Colonel; Jeremiah D. Drew of Salem, Major. Col. Whipple served as Lieut. Colonel, and Lieut. Col. Bell and Major Drew as Captains in the First Regiment. Many of the company officers and some of the men had served in the same regiment.

This regiment left Manchester for Washington on the 27th of September, 1861. As but one man from Claremont was in the Fourth, it need only be said here that it served its time, experienced many hard campaigns and much severe fighting, and leaves an honorable record.

The regiment returned to Manchester, had a handsome reception from Gov. Smyth and other citizens, and was mustered out on the 27th of August, 1865.

Corporal GEORGE H. EMERSON

Enlisted at Nashua and was mustered into Co. B, 4th Reg't, Sept. 18, 1861. Promoted to Corporal. He served his full term of enlistment and was mustered out Sept. 27, 1864. He is a son of George W. Emerson, of the 3d Reg't, formerly of Claremont.

FIFTH REGIMENT.

This regiment was organized at Concord, in September and October, 1861, under the same call and on the same bounty as the two preceding ones. The field officers were Edward E. Cross of Lancaster, Colonel; Samuel G. Langley of Manchester, Lieut. Colonel; William W. Cook of Derry, Major. Col. Cross had served in Mexico, Lieut. Col. Langley was promoted from Adjutant of the Second Regiment, and Major Cook had had some military experience. The regiment was mustered on the 26th of October, and left the State on the 28th for Bladensburg, Md., where it joined Gen. O. O. Howard's Brigade.

This regiment was recruited throughout the State. A full company was enlisted in Claremont, and mostly Claremont men, by Charles H. Long; hence a full account of its movements is important to this history.

On the 27th of November Gen. Howard's brigade marched to Alexandria, Va., joined Gen. Sumner's division, and went into winter quarters near that city, at what was called Camp California. The Fifth furnished heavy details of men during the winter for building roads, bridges, and cutting timber. The field officers established schools of instruction for the officers and sergeants, and a common school for the younger members of the regiment who needed instruction in the elementary branches.

On the 10th of March, 1862, Sumner's division left Camp California, and marched to Manassas Junction, which had been evacuated before their arrival, and they pushed on in pursuit of the retreating rebels. On the 28th the Fifth formed the advance in a reconnoissance in force on Rappahannock Station, conducted by Gen. Howard. The enemy were driven nine miles. This was the first time that the Fifth had come under fire, and the men behaved so well as to be highly commended by the General in command. From this time until the close of the war this regiment did its full share of fighting and campaigning.

On the 28th of April Col. Cross was ordered to construct a bridge across the Chickahominy, capable of bearing artillery and wagons. With his own and details from some other regiments, by the 30th, under the most difficult circumstances, they had completed what was afterward known as

"Grape-vine Bridge," seventy rods long, and in itself a prodigy of ingenuity and skill. Soon after it was the means of saving that part of the army, which, left alone on the other side, had been defeated in a pitched battle.

On the first of June occurred the battle of Fair Oaks, in which the Fifth acted a conspicuous part. In twenty minutes Col. Cross fell, wounded in the thigh, Major Cook was hit by a ball in the leg, and one hundred and eighty-six men of the regiment were killed and wounded, when the rebels gave way and left the Fifth in possession of the field. Among the killed were Charles N. Scott, James Delmage and Charles W. Wetherbee; Damon E. Hunter, mortally wounded, of Claremont, and John W. Nash of Charlestown, all of Capt. Charles H. Long's Co. G. The intensity of the musketry in this battle exceeded that of any the regiment ever heard afterward.

The regiment was in the seven days' fight, from the 25th of June to the 1st of July, and participated in the battles at Peach Orchard, Savage Station, White Oak Swamp, Charles City Cross Roads, and Malvern Hill. Gen. Sumner's corps, of which the Fifth formed a part, covered the retreat from Fair Oaks to Harrison Landing. They also covered the retreat from the second Bull Run battle, on the 29th of August, skirmishing all the way into the defenses.

At the battle of Antietam, on the 17th September, 1862, the Fifth rendered good service, and lost heavily in killed and wounded. From three hundred and nineteen officers and men who went into the fight, one hundred and eighty were killed and wounded. Corporal George Nettleton, of Claremont, although wounded, seized the fallen colors of a North-Carolina regiment and brought them off the field, for which he was promoted to a Lieutenancy. Capt. Long was wounded severely in the left arm, and Lieut. Samuel B. Little, of Claremont, received a severe flesh wound in the leg. It was during this battle that the regiment earned the name of "The Fighting Fifth."

On the 14th of November this regiment went into winter quarters at Falmouth, opposite Fredericksburg, Va., and was in the great battle of Fredericksburg on the 13th of December, where it met with a loss of one hundred and eighty-six officers and men, in killed and wounded. Among the killed from Claremont were Lieut. Charles O. Ballou, Corporal Luther A. Chase, privates Charles A. Hart, Charles D. Robinson, Chester Grinnel and Josiah S. Brown. Lieutenants Samuel B. Little and George Nettleton were mortally wounded, and both died on the 24th of the same month. Capt. J. W. Keller was badly wounded in the arm. Col. Cross was again wounded, and Major E. E. Sturtevant of Concord was killed. After this great disaster the Fifth returned to the camp at Falmouth, where it remained until the last of April, 1863.

The battle of Gettysburg occurred on the 2d and 3d of July, and the Fifth was, as usual, in the thickest of the fight. Col. Cross was killed very soon after the firing commenced. The loss of the regiment in this battle was four officers and eighty-two men killed and wounded. Among the killed from Claremont were Corporal Charles F. Burrill, James Burns, Joseph Craig, and Horace Bolio.

After this great battle, the Fifth, but a shadow of its former self, was ordered home to recruit, and arrived at Concord on the 3d of August. In about three months the regiment was recruited to its minimum strength, and the officers promoted, Lt. Col. Hapgood being commissioned Colonel. It left the State early in November, arrived at Point Lookout, Md., on the 13th, and was occupied during the winter in guarding rebel prisoners.

The other battles in which this regiment was engaged were Cold Harbor, Deep Bottom, James River, Reams' Station, Siege of Petersburg, Hatcher's Run, Five Forks, Farmville, etc.

During the summer of 1864, to October 12th, the losses to the regiment amounted to about one hundred officers and men. On this day, the Fifth having served three years, the officers who desired it, and the men who had not reënlisted, were mustered out of the service.

The Fifth was in at the death of the rebellion. It was in Gen. Miles' division, and almost constantly fighting from the last days of March until the surrender of Lee's army on the 9th of April. On the 6th this division marched thirteen miles in pursuit of the rebels, who were retreating toward Lynchburg, fought five times, captured fifteen hundred prisoners, three cannon, eleven colors, a train of near two hundred wagons, and two hundred thousand dollars of confederate money, with which the soldiers went through the farce of paying off the rebel prisoners in their hands.

After the surrender of the rebel army, the Fifth marched through Richmond to the vicinity of Washington, and in May marched in grand review before the President. It returned to Concord on the 8th of July, 1865, and was mustered out of the United States service.

CHARLES S. ABBOTT

Enlisted and was mustered into Co. G, 5th Reg't, Oct. 12, 1861. Discharged for disability April 4,

1862, and returned home. He is a son of Samuel C. Abbott of Claremont.

Lieutenant RUEL G. AUSTIN

Enlisted and was mustered into Co. G, 5th Reg't, Oct. 12, 1861. He was appointed Sergeant when the company was organized; was color sergeant at the battle of Fredericksburg, Dec. 13, 1862, where he was wounded, having his watch shot to pieces. His watch probably saved his life. On the 4th of March, 1863, he was promoted to Second Lieutenant and transferred to Co. A. At the battle of Gettysburg, July 3, 1863, he was mortally wounded; was taken to Baltimore and placed in hospital, where typhoid fever soon set in, which, with his wound, that proved more severe than was at first supposed, terminated fatally on the 26th. His funeral was attended at the Congregational Church, on Sunday the 2d of August. Lieut. Austin was born at Newport, N. H., married a daughter of Dea. Solomon Nott of Claremont, who with one child survived him, both of whom have since died. He was thirty years old and a farmer by occupation.

CHARLES H. BACON

Enlisted and was mustered into Co. G, 5th Reg't, Oct. 12, 1861. Discharged for disability Oct. 27, 1862. Son of Charles Bacon of Claremont.

FRANK BOLIO

Enlisted as a recruit, and was mustered into Co. H, 5th Reg't, Dec. 29, 1863. Wounded slightly at the battle of Cold Harbor, June 3, 1864. Deserted from McClellan Hospital, Philadelphia, February 21, 1865.

THOMAS BURNS

Enlisted and was mustered into Co. G, 5th Reg't, October 12, 1861. Was severely wounded in the hand at the battle of Fair Oaks, June 1, 1862, and again in the same hand and in the right leg at the battle of Fredericksburg, Dec. 13, 1862, and discharged on account of his wounds June 6, 1863. He is a brother of James Burns, of the same company, who was killed at the battle of Gettysburg. He was a brave soldier and is a worthy man. He is now engaged in farming at North Charlestown.

JAMES BURNS

Enlisted and was mustered into Co. G, 5th Reg't, Oct. 12, 1861. He was wounded at Fredericksburg, Dec. 13, 1862, and killed at the battle of Gettysburg, Pa., July 3, 1863, and was left upon the field. Was a younger brother of Thomas Burns, of the same company, and a good soldier.

Corporal CHARLES F. BURRILL

Enlisted and was mustered into Co. G, 5th Reg't, Oct. 12, 1861. Promoted to Corporal. Killed at the battle of Gettysburg, July 2, 1863. He was a brave and good soldier, son of Alfred Burrill of Claremont, and brother of Alfred W. Burrill of the 10th Reg't.

Sergeant GEORGE E. BROWN

Enlisted and was mustered into Co. G, 5th Reg't, Oct. 12, 1861, appointed Corporal, promoted to Sergeant, and discharged for disability Sept. 6, 1862. His record as a soldier is without a blot. He is a son of the late Edward Brown of Claremont, and a bridge builder by trade.

Corporal SAMUEL O. BENTON

Enlisted and was mustered into Co. E, 5th Reg't, Oct. 19, 1861. Promoted to Corporal. Killed at the battle of Reams' Station, Va., Aug. 16, 1864.. He was a son of William Benton of Claremont, and a brave soldier.

ALBERT W. BROWN

Enlisted as a recruit, and was mustered into Co. F, 5th Reg't, Dec. 18, 1863. Wounded severely at the battle of Cold Harbor, June 3, 1864.

JOSIAH S. BROWN

Enlisted as a recruit, and was mustered into Co. G, 5th Reg't, Aug. 11, 1862. Killed at the battle of Fredericksburg, Va., Dec. 13, 1862. He was shot through the head and died instantly. With many others of his regiment his body fell into the hands of the rebels and was never recovered. He was a brave soldier.

Corporal RALPH N. BROWN

Enlisted under Capt. Austin in April, 1861, for three months, but declined to reënlist for three years, and was discharged. Enlisted as a recruit and was mustered into Co. G, 5th Reg't, Aug. 11, 1862. Promoted to Corporal. Was severely wounded in the leg June 3, 1864, at the battle of Cold Harbor.

Corporal HOLLIS S. BROWN

Enlisted and was mustered into Co. G, 5th Reg't, Dec. 18, 1863, as a recruit. Appointed Corporal. Mustered out June 28, 1865. He was a good soldier. He is a brother of Josiah S., Ralph N., and Albert W. Brown.

HORACE BOLIO

Enlisted as a recruit, and was mustered into Co. F, 5th Reg't, Aug. 11, 1862. He was killed in the battle of Gettysburg, Pa., July 2, 1863. He was a brave soldier and always ready for duty.

JOHN BUTCHER

Enlisted as a recruit, and was mustered into Co. F, 5th Reg't, Feb. 28, 1862. Was discharged for disability Nov. 12, 1864. His disability was caused by a wound received in battle. A musket ball entered the right breast, passing through the upper portion of the right lung and coming out just below the shoulder blade. He still suffers from this wound and probably always will.

Lieutenant CHARLES O. BALLOU

Enlisted as a private under Captain Long, in August, 1861. Before the company left Claremont for the rendezvous at Concord of the Fifth Regiment, the men chose their own officers, and Mr. Ballou was elected Second Lieutenant, and received his commission from the Governor on the muster of the company, which was lettered G, on the 12th of October. Promoted to First Lieutenant Feb. 18, 1862, and assigned to Co. K. Killed at Fredericksburg, Dec. 13, 1862. He was constantly with his regiment until he was killed. While at Camp California, in the winter of 1861–62, the Fifth Regiment was attached to Gen. O. O. Howard's Brigade. In this brigade a school for officers was established, and each one was required to devote certain time to the study of military tactics and recite to their superiors at stated times. Lieut. Ballou passed the best examination, before a board of officers appointed by Gen. Howard, of any officer of his rank in the brigade. He performed every duty in camp with fidelity, and was brave and cool in battle. Capt. R. E. Cross, of his company, wrote, under date of Dec. 17, 1862: " Lieut. Ballou fell far in advance of his command, and very near the enemy's works. He was shot by one of the sharp-shooters of the enemy who occupied the rifle pits, the ball entering his neck and severing the jugular vein; he died almost instantly. He died like a soldier, loved and respected by all who knew him; and as long as the banner of the glorious Fifth continues to wave, so long shall the memory of our gallant comrade and brother officer be remembered." His body fell into the hands of the enemy and was never recovered.

Lieut. Ballou was born at Hartland, Vt., April 8, 1833, soon after which his family removed to Walpole, N. H. In the spring of 1850, his brother, John Q. A. Ballou, being home from California on a visit, Charles returned with him, and remained in California, engaged with his brother in mining operations, the culture of fruits and vegetables, and as book-keeper in a clothing store, for several years. Before going to California his education was such as he could obtain at public schools, an academy, and reading and study during all his leisure moments. While in California he became master of the Spanish language, and acted as interpreter on board vessels arriving at San Francisco. His habit of study continued to tlfe end of his life. He returned from California on account of impaired health, and made his home much of the time in Claremont with his sister, Mrs. Lewis Perry, until the breaking out of the war. He had but few confidants or intimate friends. Those who knew him best loved and respected him most.

SELWIN R. BOWMAN

Enlisted and was mustered into Co. I, 5th Reg't, Oct. 15, 1861. Discharged for disability July 22, 1862.

CHARLES D. BROUGH

Enlisted as a recruit and was mustered into Co. F, 5th Reg't, Feb. 28, 1862. He was severely wounded in the arm at the battle of Fredericksburg, Dec. 13, 1862, and was discharged, on account of wound, March 25, 1863. He showed great bravery in battle, and was a good soldier.

Lieutenant WENDELL R. COOK

Enlisted, was mustered into Co. G, 5th Reg't, Oct. 12, 1861, and immediately appointed Corporal. He was soon promoted to Sergeant, and Oct. 21, 1863, for bravery and good conduct in battle, was again promoted, to Second Lieutenant. He served the full term of his enlistment, when he was mustered out. He is a son of Wakefield Cook of Claremont. His bravery as a soldier was never questioned.

WILLIAM W. COOK

Enlisted and was mustered into Co. G, 5th Reg't, Oct. 12, 1861. Deserted Nov. 18, 1863. Apprehended Feb. 11, 1865, and deserted again April 10, 1865.

Sergeant LUTHER A. CHASE

Enlisted and was mustered into Co. G, 5th Reg't, Oct. 12, 1861. Appointed Corporal, promoted to Sergeant, and was killed at Fredericksburg, Va., Dec. 13, 1862. Soon after the battle commenced he was struck by a cannon ball near the hip, severing the limb from the body. He was immediately picked up by his companions, and died from loss of blood while they were conveying him to the hospital. He participated in eight engagements, and this was the first time he had been hit. He was about twenty years old when he enlisted, and had just graduated at Kimball Union Academy, Meriden. He was a son of Willard W. Chase of Claremont, and was much respected for his intelligence and worth by all who knew him. His funeral services were very largely attended at the Universalist Church, on Sunday, the 28th of December, Rev. Mr. Marston delivering a touching and appropriate sermon.

JOSEPH CRAIG

Enlisted and was mustered into Co. G, 5th Reg't, Oct. 12, 1861. Killed at the battle of Gettysburg, Pa., July 2, 1863. He was an Englishman by birth; when he enlisted he was employed in the Monadnock Mills. He was a brave and unflinching soldier.

SAMUEL CROWTHER

Enlisted and was mustered into Co. G, 5th Reg't, Oct. 12, 1861. He was taken prisoner at Harper's Ferry, in October, 1862, paroled in six days, exchanged in December, and returned to his regiment just after the battle of Fredericksburg. He was wounded in the right shoulder at the battle of Gettysburg, July 2, 1863, and was also shot in both legs during the second battle of Cold Harbor, June 3, 1864, and discharged at the end of his term of enlistment, Oct. 29, 1864. He was a brave soldier, always in his place in time of action. He was born at Brighton, Lancashire, England, in 1827, and came to this country several years ago.

Lieutenant ROBERT HENRY CHASE

Was mustered as a private into Co. G, 5th Reg't, Oct. 12, 1861, when eighteen years old. He was transferred to Co. C, and appointed first Sergeant, on account of his peculiar qualifications to perform the duties of the office. After the battle of Fair Oaks, June 1, 1862, which occurred in a thick wood, the Fifth Regiment having lost heavily and been driven from its position, and the rebels were supposed to have retreated, Capt. Keller called for four volunteers to go on to the battle ground and look for the wounded, when young Chase immediately stepped forward and was followed by Charles L. Severance and James Maley of Claremont, and George H. Hacket of Charlestown, who offered to go and see to their wounded friends. Severance and Maley returned unhurt, Hacket was shot in the leg while trying to raise a wounded fellow-soldier, and Chase was surprised and taken prisoner. His friends at home, learning that he was missing, supposed for a time that he was probably killed, but were soon informed that he was a prisoner. He was carried to Richmond, thence to Salisbury, N. C., where he remained about ten weeks, thence to Belle Isle, where he was paroled on the 15th of September. He was exchanged and returned to his regiment on the 14th of December, the day after the battle of Fredericksburg.

Sergeant Chase reënlisted for a second term of three years, or during the war, Jan. 1, 1864, and for meritorious conduct and bravery in action, was promoted to a Second Lieutenancy in June of the same year. He followed the fortunes of his regiment, participating in its hard marches and bloody battles, and enjoyed the confidence and esteem of officers and privates. After the severe battle at Petersburg, where the Fifth Regiment, as usual, had the post of danger and of honor, in a report of it, Major J. E. Larkin, who commanded the regiment, said — "While all did well, First Sergeant Robert H. Chase, of Co. C, seemed to his commander to merit special mention for his bravery and coolness throughout the action. Three times, through the heavy fire he carried communications to the brigade commander, and with his own hands brought cartridges from the breastworks to his company."

He was killed at the battle of Reams' Station, by a minnie ball through the neck, on the 25th of August, 1864. The Adjutant-General of New-Hampshire, in his report, speaking of the participation of the Fifth Regiment in that battle, says — "The regiment lost thirty-three of its members, among whom was Lieut. Chase, killed, a young officer lately promoted, who as Sergeant in the action of June 17th, won for himself honorable notice from the commanding officer of the regiment." The commanding officer of the regiment, in a letter to Lieut. Chase's mother, Mrs. Jotham G. Allds, informing her of the death of her son, wrote — "He was endeared to us by his noble, manly and soldierly qualities. New-Hampshire has sent no braver man to the field than Lieut. Chase. Had he lived he would soon have been promoted to Captain, a position he would have filled with honor to himself and his country." His body fell into the hands of the enemy, and was never recovered. Let his record praise him. He gave a noble young life to his country in a most holy and noble cause.

IRA D. CHENEY

Enlisted and was mustered into Co. G, 5th Reg't, Oct. 12, 1861. He was most of his term sick in hospital, saw but little service, was discharged July 11, 1862, returned home, and is now employed in Monadnock Mills.

ELIJAH S. CARLETON

Enlisted and was mustered into Co. G, 5th Reg't, Oct. 12, 1861. Wounded in the shoulder by a spent ball, and disabled at Fredericksburg, Dec. 13, 1862. Transferred to Veteran Reserve Corps, July 1, 1863; served to the end of his term of enlistment, and was discharged in October, 1864. He is a son of Stephen Carleton of Claremont, was twenty-seven years old when discharged, and now lives in Worcester, Mass.

DANIEL CUMMINGS

Enlisted and was mustered into Co. G, 5th Reg't, Oct. 12, 1861. He served his full term of enlistment, following the fortunes of his regiment, was mustered out Oct. 29, 1864, and returned home.

LYMAN H. CONE

Enlisted and was mustered into Co. G, 5th Reg't, Oct. 12, 1861. Was mustered out at the end of his term of enlistment, Oct. 29, 1864, and returned home. Was a good soldier.

CHARLES F. COLSTON

Enlisted under Capt. Austin in April, 1861, for three months, was rejected by the examining surgeon at Portsmouth, and returned home. He enlisted again, was mustered into Co. G, 5th Reg't, Oct. 12, 1861, and discharged for disability Jan. 20, 1863. He subsequently enlisted in the navy, and died in 1866.

JAMES DELMAGE

Enlisted under Capt. Austin in April, 1861, for three months, and declining to enlist for three years, was discharged. He enlisted again and was mustered into Co. G, 5th Reg't, Oct. 12, 1861. At the battle of Fair Oaks, June 1, 1862, he was killed instantly by a minnie ball, by the same volley that killed Charles N. Scott, and John W. Nash, and mortally wounded Charles W. Wetherbee. He was buried by his fellow-soldiers in the same grave with them. Mr. Delmage was born in Champlain, N. Y., in 1824, and came to Claremont in 1858. He was a brave and faithful soldier, and left a wife and two young children.

GEORGE W. FAIRBANKS

Enlisted and was mustered into Co. G, 5th Reg't, Oct. 12, 1861. Discharged for disability Sept. 6,

1862. Enlisted into the Veteran Reserve Corps, Dec. 30, 1863, served to the end of the war and was mustered out Nov. 7, 1865.

JAMES S. A. GATES

Enlisted and was mustered into Co. G, 5th Reg't, Oct. 12, 1861. Discharged for disability Sept. 3, 1862. He is a son of the late James M. Gates of Claremont.

ISRAEL GERMARSH

Enlisted as a recruit, and was mustered into Co. G, 5th Reg't, April 20, 1862. Deserted in August, 1863.

LEMUEL A. GILES

Enlisted and was mustered into Co. G, 5th Reg't, Oct. 12, 1861. Severely wounded in the thigh. Served his full time, was in several battles, and mustered out Oct. 29, 1864.

CHESTER F. GRINNELS

Enlisted as a recruit, and was mustered into Co. G, 5th Reg't, Sept. 17, 1862. Killed at Fredericksburg, Va., Dec. 13, 1862. He left a young widow. Before his enlistment he was employed in the Monadnock Mills. His body fell into the hands of the enemy and was never recovered.

CHARLES B. HART

Enlisted and was mustered into Co. G, 5th Reg't, Oct. 12, 1861. Discharged for disability Nov. 29, 1862. Enlisted into the Veteran Reserve Corps, at Concord, Aug. 30, 1864, for three years.

CHARLES A. HART

Enlisted and was mustered into Co. G, 5th Reg't, Oct. 12, 1861. Wounded at the battle of Fair Oaks, June 1, 1862. A minnie ball entered the thigh and was taken out four days afterward. He was in the battle of Antietam, and others, where the Fifth was engaged, always behaving bravely. At the battle of Fredericksburg, Dec. 13, 1862, he was mortally wounded, and left upon the field. When our men, under a flag of truce, went to take care of the wounded and bury the dead, they found Hart and Luther A. Chase, of the same company, side by side, both alive. When the men were considering which to take first, Hart raised himself on his side, looked at his wound, then at Chase, whose leg was shot away, and said, "Leave me here for I shall soon die, but take care of Luther." He was a son of Josiah Hart of Claremont, nineteen years old, and all agree that he was one of the best soldiers in his company. He was buried upon the field.

LEANDER HARRIMAN

Enlisted as a recruit, and was mustered into Co. G, 5th Reg't, Sept. 17, 1862. Transferred to the Veteran Reserve Corps, Sept. 1, 1863.

SAMUEL HENRY

Enlisted and was mustered into Co. G, 5th Reg't, Oct. 12, 1861. Discharged for disability Sept. 3, 1862. Enlisted into the Veteran Reserve Corps Aug. 21, 1863. Mustered out Nov. 7, 1865.

ELISHA M. HILL

Enlisted as a recruit, and was mustered into Co. G, 5th Reg't, Feb. 28, 1862. Wounded. Died of wounds Oct. 27, 1862.

DAMON E. HUNTER

Enlisted and was mustered into Co. G, 5th Reg't, Oct. 12, 1861. Mortally wounded at the battle of Fair Oaks, Va., June 1, 1862, losing a leg and an arm, and died in hospital of wounds June 22, 1862, and was buried at Yorktown.

Sergeant LEVI JOHNSON

Enlisted as a recruit, and was mustered into Co. G, 5th Reg't, Aug. 20, 1862. He joined the regiment at Antietam, just after the battle there. He was in the battles of Fredericksburg, Chancellorsville, and others where the Fifth was engaged up to August, 1863, when he was detailed to the commissary department, and appointed Commissary Sergeant Jan. 15, 1865. Served to the end of the war, and was mustered out May 30, 1865, under a special order of the War Department.

Captain JACOB W. KELLER

First enlisted in the Sixth Massachusetts Regiment for three months, and was with it when it was assaulted by the mob in the streets of Baltimore, on the 19th of April, 1861. At the end of his term of enlistment he returned to Claremont, the home of his adoption. He enlisted again in August, under Capt. Long, was chosen First Lieutenant of his company, which was attached to the Fifth New-Hampshire Regiment and lettered G, and commissioned by the Governor Oct. 12, 1861. Promoted to Captain July 26, 1862. Wounded severely in the arm at the battle of Fredericksburg, Dec. 13, 1862, and was honorably discharged Jan. 26, 1864. He was subsequently appointed Captain in the Veteran Reserve Corps, and after the close of the war was commissioned First Lieutenant in the regular army. Capt. Keller came to this country from Germany about the year 1855, worked on the farm of Capt. Charles F. Long for a time, and then learned the trade of a machinist at the shop of J. P. Upham & Co., and went to Boston, where he was living at the time the war broke out. He is a worthy man and one of the best officers in his regiment.

JOSEPH W. KELLEY

Enlisted and was mustered into Co. G, 5th Reg't, Oct. 12, 1861. He was taken sick near Yorktown, and died on the passage from Fortress Monroe to Washington, in May, 1862. He was about twenty-one years old, a farmer by occupation, a good soldier, and a worthy young man. He leaves parents and one sister, living in Cornish, near to Claremont line.

DAVID H. LATERMOULLE

Enlisted as a recruit, Jan. 4, 1864. Wounded June 3, 1864. Transferred to Veteran Reserve Corps Jan. 24, 1865.

Lieutenant SAMUEL BROWN LITTLE

Second Lieutenant Co. G, 5th Regiment New-Hampshire Volunteer Infantry, was born at Newburyport, Essex County, Mass., July 24, 1828, and was the youngest of a family of six boys, who, on account of the improvidence of the father, were wholly dependent for support upon the industry and energy of a most excellent mother. She died when Samuel was but eight months old, leaving the six boys — the oldest having barely past his seventh year — to the cold charity of the world. When ten years old, Samuel went to live with a farmer, and from that time earned his own support. He worked upon the farm — attending the public schools about three months each year — until he was sixteen, when he went to learn the trade of a house painter. At eighteen he went into business for himself at Brookline, Mass., where he remained most of the time until August 1856, when he removed to Claremont, Sullivan County, New-Hampshire, where two of his brothers had married and settled. Samuel was married in November, 1849, to Mary L. Gould of Brighton, Mass.

Soon after his removal to Claremont, Samuel entered into a copartnership with his brother, Joseph T. Little, and they carried on the business of house painting until September, 1861, when he enlisted under the call of President Lincoln for three hundred thousand volunteers for three years or during the war, as a private in the 5th Regiment

New-Hampshire Volunteers. At that time all the bounty offered was ten dollars from the State. Mr. Little was mustered into the United States service at Concord on the 17th of October, 1861, and immediately appointed First Sergeant of Co. G, which had been recruited at Claremont.

On the 1st of August, 1862, for bravery and meritorious conduct, Sergeant Little was promoted to a Lieutenancy in his regiment, and remained with Co. G, where he enjoyed the confidence and esteem of the officers and men.

At the battle of Antietam, September 17, 1862. Lieutenant Little was in the thickest of the fight. His Captain, Long, was soon wounded, and Lieut. Little was in command of the company. In the course of the day he received a severe flesh wound in the thigh, which disabled him for duty, and he soon after came home on a furlough. During his absence his regiment had moved to Falmouth, opposite Fredericksburg, where a battle was impending, and Lieut. Little determined if possible to bear a part in it. And then, his brother, Moses C. Little, of the 19th Massachusetts was there, and he wished to be near him. Impelled by these considerations, before the expiration of his leave, when yet suffering from the wound received at Antietam, and against the advice of his physician, he left home on the 8th of December, and after traveling as rapidly as possible, rejoined his regiment but one hour before the opening of the great battle of Fredericksburg on the 13th. He found that his brother Moses had been killed by a rebel sharpshooter, on the 11th, while assisting to build pontoon bridges across the Rappahannock river.

His Colonel, Edward E. Cross, and other officers, seeing the feeble state Lieut. Little was in, tried to dissuade him from going into the battle, but he persisted. Very soon after the fight commenced, his Captain, Jacob W. Keller, was severely wounded and carried to the rear, when Lieut. Little sprang to the command of his company, and as he was cheering his men forward, with his sword above his head, he received a wound in the leg, and another — the fatal one — in his shoulder. A minnie ball entered the body at the shoulder and did not pass out. He was carried to the Lacey House, Falmouth, where, after great suffering, which he bore patiently, he died on the 24th.

Lieut. Little's remains were brought to Claremont and buried by Hiram Lodge of Free and Accepted Masons, of which he was an honored and beloved brother, with appropriate ceremonies. He was an active and worthy member of the Universalist Church and Society — always in his place —

and a leader in the Sunday School. His funeral was very largely attended by citizens of Claremont, in the Town Hall. His friend and pastor, Rev. Mr. Marston, preached a most appropriate and impressive sermon from the text found in Revelations, 14th chapter and 13th verse :

"Blessed are the dead which die in the Lord from henceforth : Yea, saith the Spirit, that they may rest from their labors; and their works do follow them."

Lieut. Little entered the army from a true sense of duty, and laid his life upon the altar of his country a sacrifice to universal liberty and justice.

Thus died and was buried a most noble, patriotic and brave soldier; an upright and respected citizen; a kind and affectionate brother, and a devoted, loving and beloved husband.

Lieutenant JOHN W. LAWRENCE

Enlisted under Capt. Austin in April, 1861, for three months; was chosen First Lieutenant of the Claremont company; went to Portsmouth, where the company was broken up, and declining to reënlist for three years, was discharged. The following September he enlisted at Newport, was mustered into Co. E, 5th Reg't, Oct. 19, 1861, and appointed Sergeant. Feb. 16, 1862, he was promoted to Second Lieutenant, was wounded in the battle of Malvern Hill, July 3, 1862, and resigned, on account of disability occasioned by his wound, Oct. 23, 1862.

RUSSELL LOVEJOY

Enlisted and was mustered into Co. G, 5th Reg't, Oct. 12, 1861. Discharged for disability Feb. 28, 1863. Enlisted into the Veteran Reserve Corps Aug. 30, 1864, and served to the end of the war, and was mustered out Nov. 7, 1865.

ADDISON P. MOORE

Enlisted and was mustered into Co. G, 5th Reg't, Oct. 12, 1861. Discharged for disability Oct. 20, 1862, and came home. He is a son of Curtis Moore of Claremont, and brother of Horatio C. Moore of the 3d Reg't, who was killed at James Island.

JAMES P. MILTON

Enlisted and was mustered into Co. G, 5th Reg't, Oct. 12, 1861. Discharged for disability March 24, 1862. He came home with a fatal disease upon him, and died July 27, 1866. He was a son of John M. Milton of Claremont, and brother of Dr. Charles A. Milton, who, as Medical Cadet, died at Mound City, Ill.

JAMES MALEY

Enlisted and was mustered into Co. G, 5th Reg't, Oct. 12, 1861. Wounded severely at the battle of Fredericksburg, Dec. 13, 1862, and was discharged Feb. 28, 1863, on account of wounds. Enlisted into Co. A, Heavy Artillery, and was mustered May 26, 1863, served to the end of the war, and was mustered out with the regiment. He was a brave soldier.

FRANK E. MARSH

Enlisted and was mustered into Co. G, 5th Reg't, Oct. 12, 1861. He served faithfully as wagoner during the entire term of his enlistment, was mustered out October 29, 1864, and returned to his home in Claremont where he still resides. He is a son of Dr. E. C. Marsh of the New-Hampshire Cavalry.

GEORGE W. MOODY

Enlisted as a musician, and was mustered into Co. G, 5th Reg't, Oct. 12, 1861. Discharged Aug. 28, 1862, and returned to his home in Claremont. He is a son of Jonathan Moody.

Sergeant BARON S. NOYES

Enlisted in Capt. Austin's company in April, 1861; went to Portsmouth where most of the men reënlisted for three years, but he declined to do so, and was sent to Fort Constitution, where he served out his term of enlistment. He enlisted again, was mustered into Co. E, 5th Reg't, Oct. 19, 1861, and appointed Sergeant. Discharged for disability March 4, 1863. September 9, 1864, he again enlisted in the United States Invalid Corps, at Concord, and was mustered out Nov. 14, 1865. Since then he has lived in Claremont. His officers speak of him as a good soldier in field and camp.

ENOS B. NEVERS

Enlisted and was mustered into Co. I, 5th Reg't, Oct. 15, 1861. Deserted Aug. 30, 1862.

DANIEL J. NEVERS

Enlisted as a recruit, and was mustered into Co. I, 5th Reg't, Feb. 28, 1862. Discharged Dec. 12, 1862. Enlisted into the Veteran Reserve Corps, Dec. 29, 1863, where he served to the end of the war.

CHARLES H. NEVERS

Enlisted and was mustered into Co. G, 5th Reg't, Oct. 12, 1861. He was killed in battle at White Oak Swamp, Va., June 30, 1862.

DAVID H. NICHOLS

Enlisted and was mustered into Co. G, 5th Reg't, Oct. 12, 1861. Discharged for disability Feb. 18, 1863. Enlisted into the Veteran Reserve Corps Aug. 25, 1864, and was discharged for disability May 6, 1865.

Lieutenant GEORGE NETTLETON

Enlisted as a private and was mustered into Co. G, 5th Reg't, Oct. 12, 1861. He was promoted to Sergeant, and afterward, Nov. 11, 1862, for bravery in action, was promoted to Second Lieutenant. He was mortally wounded at the battle of Fredericksburg, Va., Dec. 13, 1862, and died of his wounds at the Ninth Army Corps Hospital, on the 23d. Lieut. Nettleton was a native of England, came to this country in 1857, and settled in Claremont, with his family. He enlisted from a sense of duty, and proved himself a brave soldier. At the battle of Antietam, Sept. 17, 1862, he was struck by a shell, but not very much hurt, after which, during the battle, he captured the colors of the 4th North-Carolina Regiment and brought them from the field. The colors were sent to the Governor of this State and are now deposited with other trophies of the war, at the State House. For this act and for meritorious conduct generally, he was commissioned Second Lieutenant. At the battle of Fredericksburg, as he was leading his company, several men carrying the colors of his regiment were shot down, when Lieut. Nettleton seized and had but just raised them when he was hit by a grape shot in the thigh and a minnie ball in the bowels, mortally wounding him. A short time before this battle, in a letter to his wife, he wrote, "I may fall, but ever remember it was at the post of duty, and in a noble cause." His remains were brought home with those of Lieut. Little, and buried, Rev. Mr. Hartwell preaching an appropriate sermon. He left a wife and two young children.

Sergeant WILLIAM H. NUTT

Enlisted and was mustered into Co. G, 5th Reg't, Oct. 12, 1861. He was for a time sick in hospital at New-York, and was afterward for several months on duty at Fort Hamilton. Transferred to Battery G, 5th United States Artillery, Oct. 28, 1863, which was assigned to Gen. Banks' expedition, and went to New-Orleans. He reënlisted in the spring of 1864, and was appointed Corporal, and afterward promoted to Quartermaster-Sergeant. His battery was engaged in the siege of Port Hudson, and the first to enter the Fort. He was in thirteen different engagements, and never received a severe wound. He was mustered out after the close of the war, at Little Rock, Ark., where he married and is now settled.

ANDREW J. PIERCE

Enlisted and was mustered into Co. G, 5th Reg't, Oct. 12, 1861. Discharged for disability at Annapolis, Md., Oct. 28, 1862, and returned home. He is a paper-maker by trade, and son of June Pierce of Claremont.

Corporal GEORGE H. PUTNAM

Enlisted and was mustered into Co. G, 5th Reg't, Oct. 12, 1861. Killed at the battle of Cold Harbor, Va., June 3, 1864. In the morning of that day, being aware of the impending battle, he said to a friend — " I know I shall not come out of that fight alive." He had been in every battle where his regiment was engaged — Yorktown, Fair Oaks, Savage Station, Peach Orchard, White Oak Swamp, Charles City Cross Roads, Malvern Hill, Antietam, Fredericksburg, Chancellorsville, Gettysburg and Cold Harbor. He was slightly wounded at the battle of Gettysburg, but was only absent from his company one day. He was always cheerful in the performance of every duty, a cool, brave and patriotic soldier, enjoying alike the esteem and confidence of officers and privates. He went to the war from a high sense of duty, and gave his life to his country. Corporal Putnam was born in Claremont in 1840, son of the late Zelotes Putnam, and brother of Charles E. Putnam of the 2d Reg't, who was killed at Williamsburg.

JOEL W. PATRICK

Enlisted and was mustered into Co. G, 5th Reg't, Oct. 12, 1861. Soon after his regiment went into camp near Washington he was detailed for signal service, a position of responsibility, the duties of which he is said to have performed acceptably. In July, 1862, he came home on a furlough, was taken down with camp-fever, which assumed a typhoid type, and died at the residence of his father, William Patrick, on the 15th of August. His funeral was largely attended at the Baptist church, Rev. Mr. Ayer preaching an appropriate sermon. At the time of his death he was twenty-eight years old, and brother of Henry W. Patrick of the 2d Reg't and Lieut. Charles E. Patrick of the New-Hampshire Cavalry.

Corporal EDWARD P. PIKE

Enlisted and was mustered into Co. G, 5th Reg't, Oct. 12, 1861. Appointed Corporal, served the full term of his enlistment, and was mustered out Oct. 29, 1864. He was in many battles with his regiment, returned home without a wound, and now lives in California.

Sergeant WILLIAM E. PARRISH

Enlisted at Claremont, under Capt. Austin, for three months; went to Portsmouth and reënlisted for three years; was mustered into Co. F, 2d Reg't, June 4, 1861, and discharged for disability July 31, 1861. He enlisted again in Capt. Long's Co. G, 5th Reg't, was mustered Oct. 12, 1861, and appointed Sergeant. He was discharged again for disability September 6, 1862. After recovering he went to St. Johnsbury, Vt., was drafted and put into the 4th Vermont Volunteers. In the battle of the Wilderness he was wounded three or four times, taken prisoner, sent to Libby prison, Richmond, and from there to Andersonville, since which nothing is known of him or his fate. He was a son of the late Thomas D. Parrish of this town, and a brother of Lyman F. of the 2d Regiment, Thomas D. of the 26th Mass. and James C. of the 5th N. H. Reg't.

JAMES C. PARRISH

Enlisted and was mustered into Co. H, 5th Reg't, Oct. 19, 1861. Reënlisted Jan. 1, 1864. He was severely wounded in the foot, and was discharged. He is a brother of Lyman F., William E. and Thomas D. Parrish, and now lives in Canada.

JOHN J. PRENTISS, Jr.

Enlisted and was mustered into Co. G, 5th Reg't, Oct. 12, 1861. He was discharged Nov. 23, 1863, by reason of an appointment to a Second Lieutenancy in the First New-Hampshire Cavalry, which position he was never called to fill. While in the 5th Regiment he was in many battles, and proved himself a brave and good soldier. He is a brother of Capt. William P. Prentiss of the New-Hampshire Cavalry.

CHARLES H. PARMALEE

Enlisted under Capt. Austin in April, 1861, for three months, and served out the term of his enlistment at Fort Constitution. He was drafted at West Lebanon, Aug. 27, 1863, and mustered into Co. F, 5th Reg't, Oct. 10, 1863. Missing April 7, 1865. Gained from missing and was mustered out June 28, 1865. He is brother of Edward A. Parmalee.

EDWARD A. PARMALEE,

Drafted at West Lebanon, Aug. 27, 1863, and was mustered into Co. F, 5th Reg't, Oct. 10, 1863.

Wounded severely in the foot near Hatcher's Run, Va., March 25, 1865, and was taken prisoner. His foot was amputated at the instep by a rebel surgeon in their field hospital, after which he was sent to Libby Prison, where he remained two days and was paroled and sent to Annapolis, Md. His foot healed and he was honorably discharged on the 26th of June, 1865, and came home. He is a brother of Charles H. Parmalee of the same company.

JULIUS B. PAUL

Enlisted and was mustered into Co. G, 5th Reg't, Oct. 12, 1861. Transferred to the Veteran Reserve Corps July 1, 1863, where he served to the end of the war. He was a brave and faithful soldier.

JOHN D. ROBERTS

Enlisted and was mustered into Co. G, 5th Reg't, Oct. 12, 1861. Discharged Oct. 28, 1862.

CHARLES D. ROBINSON

Enlisted as a recruit, and was mustered into Co. G, 5th Reg't, Sept. 18, 1862. Killed at the battle of Fredericksburg, Va., Dec. 13, 1862. He was the only son of Dean D. Robinson, who came from Acworth to Claremont a few years since, and now lives in Maryland.

HENRY L. ROWELL

Enlisted and was mustered into Co. G, 5th Reg't, Oct. 12, 1861. Discharged for disability, March 25, 1862. He is a son of the late James E. Rowell of Claremont, and brother of George E. Rowell of the 10th Regiment.

LEVI F. REED

Enlisted and was mustered into Co. G, 5th Reg't, Oct, 12, 1861. Discharged for disability Nov. 26, 1862. Enlisted into the Veteran Reserve Corps Aug. 30, 1864, and was discharged Nov. 7, 1865.

GEORGE READ

Enlisted and was mustered into Co. G, 5th Reg't, Oct. 12, 1861. He died at Newark, N. J., in the United States Hospital, of chronic diarrhea, Sept. 9, 1862. He was in most of the battles in which his regiment participated, until his last sickness, among which were those of Fair Oaks, the Seven Days Fight, the Wilderness, and others. He was the oldest son of the late Jonathan Read of Claremont, and brother of J. Parker Read of the 2d Regiment. On hearing of his sickness his mother went immediately to him, but he died an hour before her arrival. She took his remains and started for home, arriving here on a beautiful moonlight night. A procession was formed at the railroad station, and marched to the cemetery, where, in the shades of night, they were buried with appropriate ceremonies, conducted by Rev. R. F. Lawrence. The scene and the occasion were most solemn and impressive, long to be remembered by those who witnessed it. On the following Sabbath, Rev. Mr. Lawrence preached a funeral sermon to a large and interested audience, taking for his text these words of the Psalmist: "How long, Lord? Wilt thou be angry for ever?" At the time of his death young Read was nineteen years old; was a kind and obedient son and an affectionate and beloved brother. He left behind him a widowed mother, one brother — J. Parker Read of the 2d Regiment, — four sisters, and many friends who deeply mourn his early death.

DAVID R. ROYS

Enlisted and was mustered into Co. G, 5th Reg't, Oct. 12, 1861. He was the first in his regiment to reënlist for a second term of three years. Served as private and bugler in his regiment, and as bugler at Head-quarters of Gen. Hinks' colored brigade, and orderly at Brigade Head-quarters. At the battle of Antietam his belt-plate was hit and broken by a minnie ball. The ball passed through the plate, two thicknesses of leather and his clothing and lodged. His belt-plate undoubtedly saved his life on that occasion. The ball did not leave a scratch on his person, though he was injured internally, but not severely. He was in the siege of Yorktown, the battles of Fair Oaks, Peach Orchard, Savage Station, Charles City Cross Roads, Malvern Hill, Antietam, Fredericksburg, Chancellorsville, Gettysburg, Wilson's Landing, siege of Petersburg, and at the surrender of Lee's army. Great confidence was reposed in him by his officers, for his intelligence, fidelity and courage. He was mustered out July 8, 1865, came home, and is now employed at the Home Mill. He is a son of Henry Roys of Claremont, and brother of Henry F. Roys of the 2d Regiment.

CHARLES N. SCOTT

Enlisted and was mustered into Co. G, 5th Reg't, Oct. 12, 1861. He was killed at the battle of Fair Oaks, June 1, 1862, by the same volley that killed Charles W. Wetherbee, James Delmage and John W. Nash, and was buried in the same grave with them, by his fellow-soldiers. He was born at Springfield, Vt., April 18, 1836, and came to Claremont with his parents in 1849. He was an intelligent, industrious and worthy citizen, and a brave and faithful soldier, respected alike by officers and men of his regiment. For some years before the rebellion broke out he had been employed upon the farm of Capt. Charles F. Long. After his death two of his brothers enlisted in the 9th Vermont Regiment, one of whom died of wounds received at the battle of Chancellorsville, and the other died of disease contracted in the service. Another brother enlisted in an Ohio regiment, where he served until after the end of the war, and was honorably discharged. Soon after enlisting Mr. Scott was married, and left a widow but no children.

WILLIAM S. STURTEVANT

Was drafted at West Lebanon, Aug. 27, 1863, and mustered into Co. F, 5th Reg't, Oct. 10, 1863. Mustered out June 28, 1865.

ELISHA S. SHOLES

Enlisted and was mustered into Co. G, 5th Reg't, Oct. 12, 1861. Wounded severely in the right side, and again by a buck-shot in the leg above the knee, at the battle of Fredericksburg, Dec. 13, 1862. Discharged on account of wounds, April 2, 1863. Enlisted in the Veteran Reserve Corps Sept. 12, 1863, and was on duty at West Lebanon and Concord until Nov. 13, 1865, when he was mustered out.

CHARLES E. SEVERANCE

Enlisted and was mustered into Co. G, 5th Reg't, Oct. 12, 1861. Transferred to Veteran Reserve Corps July 1, 1863, on account of wound received in the knee at the battle of Fair Oaks, June 1, 1862.

CHARLES L. SEVERANCE

Enlisted and was mustered into Co. G, 5th Reg't, Oct. 12, 1861. Wounded in the thigh, at the battle of Antietam, Sept. 17, 1862. Transferred to Veteran Reserve Corps July 1, 1863. Mustered out at the end of his term of enlistment, Oct., 1864. He still carries the ball in his thigh.

HENRY S. SILSBEE

Enlisted as a recruit, and was mustered into Co. G, 5th Reg't, Aug. 14, 1862. Was wounded at the battle of Fredericksburg, and subsequently transferred to the Veteran Reserve Corps, where he served until after the end of the war. He is a son of Solon Silsbee of Claremont.

CORNELIUS H. STONE

Enlisted and was mustered into Co. F, 5th Reg't, as a recruit, February 28, 1862, followed the fortunes of the regiment until July 26, 1863, when he was taken prisoner at White Plains, Va., carried to Libby Prison, Richmond, searched and relieved of all valuables, and then taken to Belle Isle, where he was kept one hundred and fourteen days, when he was paroled, and finally exchanged May 28, 1864. He reënlisted April 1, 1864. He was in the battle of Cold Harbor, June 3, 1864, where he received six wounds — one through the right arm with a minnie ball, breaking it badly; three in the left leg, two with minnie balls below the knee, and a grape shot in the knee; a minnie ball in the right side, and a piece of shell in the back. He laid in a rifle-pit on the battle-field, in the hands of the rebels, with nothing to eat or drink, from the 3d to the 9th, when the rebels were driven back and the ground retaken by our men. At night our men built breastworks to within about two rods of where Stone laid so weak from his sufferings and the loss of blood that he could hardly speak or move. Under cover of darkness he crawled with the utmost difficulty into the intrenchments and fell into the hands of the second Delaware regiment. The rebels took from him fifty dollars, his veteran discharge paper, and all the other valuables he had in his pockets, even to his tobacco. His wounds were dressed on the morning of the 10th, and he was carried to White House Landing, Va., riding fourteen miles over corduroy roads in an army wagon. From there he was carried to Mansion House Hospital, Alexandria, where his leg was amputated above the knee. He remained there until the 19th of November, his leg being nearly healed, when he was sent to Pemberton Square Hospital, Boston. After he reached Boston, and was hobbling along Tremont street toward the hospital, his crutch slipped on the sidewalk and he fell, injuring his leg very seriously. He afterward took cold in it and gangrene set in, which was not overcome under several weeks, and when it was it had eaten off the main arteries, and four inches more of his leg had to be amputated. The physician told Stone and his friends that he probably could not live through the operation, though he could not possibly live without it. It took an hour and a half to perform the operation. He did live, however, and six weeks afterward was sent to the Military Hospital at Manchester, this State, and subsequently to Central Park Hospital, New-York, where he was furnished with an artificial leg by the Government, and was discharged on the 8th of June, 1865. He subsequently fully recovered and was able to labor daily. Very few men suffered so much for their country as did young Stone. His Colonel, Hapgood, said he was one of the bravest and best soldiers in his regiment.

ROLAND TAYLOR

Enlisted and was mustered into Co. G, 5th Reg't, Oct. 12, 1861. Mortally wounded at the battle of Gettysburg, July 2, 1862, and died a few days afterward. He came to Claremont but a few months before he enlisted and worked in the Monadnock Mills. He is spoken of as a brave soldier.

SAMUEL J. THORNING

Enlisted as a recruit, and was mustered into Co. F, 5th Reg't, April 20, 1862. He experienced great hardship and fatigue in the seven days' battle, in June, and contracted disease which terminated in epilepsy, from which he never has recovered. He was discharged Jan. 15, 1863, and returned home a perfect wreck.

Corporal MATTHEW T. TOWNE

Enlisted under Capt. Austin, in April, 1861, for three months, and served out his term of enlistment at Fort Constitution. Enlisted again and was mustered into Co. E, 5th Reg't, Oct. 19, 1861. Promoted to Corporal. He distinguished himself as Corporal of the Regimental Pioneer Corps,

7*

building corduroy roads, bridges, &c. Discharged for disability Dec. 24, 1862. In September, 1863, he was hooked in the abdomen by a cow which he was leading, and so much injured that he died the next day. He was a son of David Towne, and brother of Samuel C. Towne of the 9th Regiment.

Sergeant SYLVANUS M. TYRRELL

Enlisted and was mustered into Co. G, 5th Reg't, Oct. 12, 1861. Appointed Sergeant; served his full term of enlistment, and was mustered out Oct. 29, 1864.

CHESTER F. TIBBELS

Enlisted and was mustered into Co. G, 5th Reg't, Oct. 12, 1861. Discharged for disability April 22, 1864. He enlisted under Capt. Austin, in April, 1861, for three months, but did not reënlist for three years and was discharged.

Corporal LUCIUS VEASEY

Enlisted and was mustered into Co. G, 5th Reg't, Oct. 12, 1861, and appointed Corporal. He was severely wounded in the head at the battle of Antietam, Sept. 17, 1862, from which he has not and probably never will recover. Discharged for disability April 13, 1863.

HARVEY M. WAKEFIELD

Enlisted and was mustered into Co. G, 5th Reg't, Oct. 12, 1861. Died in hospital July 5, 1862. He left a widow and three young children to mourn his loss. He came to Claremont from Vermont six or eight years before his enlistment.

Sergeant CHARLES W. WETHERBEE

Enlisted under Capt. Austin, in April, 1861, for three months; went to Portsmouth, reënlisted for three years and was mustered into Co. H, 2d Reg't, June 5, 1861. He was in the first battle of Bull Run, soon after which he was discharged for disability. He enlisted again and was mustered into Co. G, 5th Reg't, Oct. 12, 1861. Appointed Sergeant on the organization of the company. At the battle of Fair Oaks, Va., June 1, 1862, he was fatally wounded in the head by a minnie ball and died the next day. He was buried by his fellow-soldiers in the same grave with Charles N. Scott and James Delmage of Claremont, and John W. Nash of Charlestown, all members of the same company. Scott, Delmage and Nash were instantly killed at the same time that Wetherbee was mortally wounded. Lieut. Keller, in a letter to his wife, wrote—"Your husband fell fighting nobly for his country. We all mourn his loss, and you have the heart-felt sympathy of all." Sergeant Wetherbee was born at Alstead, this State, March 4, 1828, and removed with his family to this town about three years before the breaking out of the rebellion. His record as a soldier stands well. He left a widow and two daughters, six and eleven years old. The youngest daughter died of diphtheria in June, 1865.

NELSON WHITMORE

Enlisted as a recruit, and was mustered into Co. G, 5th Reg't, Sept. 17, 1862. Wounded severely in the leg and was subsequently discharged on account of wounds. Enlisted into Veteran Reserve Corps Aug. 25, 1864. Mustered out Nov. 7, 1865. While in the 5th Reg't he showed great bravery and coolness in action.

LUCIUS C. WEBB

Enlisted and was mustered into Co. G, 5th Reg't, Oct. 12, 1861. In the winter of 1863, on account of sickness caused by exposure, he was sent to hospital where he was discharged April 18, 1863. After his discharge he was for a time servant for Gen. Marston, and subsequently, when driving a sutler's wagon, was taken prisoner, with two others, by Moseby's Guerrillas, and escaped after being with them six weeks, riding away one of their best horses. He is a son of George O. Webb of the same company.

GEORGE O. WEBB

Enlisted and was mustered into Co. G, 5th Reg't, Oct. 12, 1861. Died suddenly at Camp Fair Oaks, Va., June 15, 1862. He had been unwell for a few days, but was able to be about up to the hour of his death. He was taken in a fit and did not speak to those who were with him. He was buried by his comrades near where he died. He left a widow and three sons, one of whom, Lucius C., was a member of the same company. He came to Claremont in 1843, and at the time of his enlistment was in the employ of J. P. Upham & Co.

FRANK YOUNG

Enlisted as a recruit, and was mustered into Co. F, 5th Reg't, Feb. 28, 1862. Served until the end of the war, and was mustered out with his regiment. He is a brother of John E. Young of Co. G, same regiment.

JOHN E. YOUNG

Enlisted, was mustered into Co. G, 5th Reg't, Oct. 12, 1861. Promoted to Corporal. Promoted to Sergeant. Wounded, June 3, 1864, in the battle of Cold Harbor. Mustered out at the end of his term of enlistment, Oct. 29, 1864. Brother of Frank Young of Co. F, same regiment.

SIXTH REGIMENT.

This regiment was recruited mainly in the western part of the State, and was organized at Keene. Claremont had just furnished nearly a full company for the Fifth, and but few men from Claremont entered the Sixth. The field officers were, Nelson Converse of Marlborough, Colonel; Simon G. Griffin of Concord, Lieut. Colonel, and Charles Scott of Peterborough, Major. Lieut. Col. Griffin was promoted from Captain in the 2d New-Hampshire Regiment.

The muster of the regiment was completed on the 30th of November, 1861, and it left the State on the 25th of December for Washington, and was assigned to Burnside's expedition. It suffered considerable loss from sickness during the winter. On the 7th of April, 1862, the brigade to which this regiment was attached being encamped at Roanoke Island, Lieut. Col. Griffin was ordered to take four companies from his regiment and two from the New-York 9th and break up an encampment at Elizabeth City, N. C., where a rebel regiment was being organized. They attacked the camp on the morning of the 8th, killed one man, wounded two, took seventy-four prisoners, while the remainder of the rebels took to the woods. They also captured three hundred and fifty stand of arms, a quantity of ammunition and other property, and completely broke up this haunt of the rebels.

On the 19th of April, the regiment signalized itself for discipline and bravery in the demonstration on Norfolk. Gen. Burnside complimented it, and issued an order that it inscribe upon its colors "Camden, April 19, 1862." Early in August the Sixth joined the army of Gen. Pope at Culpeper Court House, and was in the disastrous campaign which followed, evincing good pluck and endurance. It was in the thickest of the fight at the second Bull Run battle, August 29th, and out of four hundred and fifty officers and men who went into the battle, thirty-two were killed, one hundred and ten wounded, and sixty-eight missing, making a total of two hundred and ten. It was also in the skirmishes and battles that followed on the 30th, 31st, and the 1st of September.

This regiment was at the battle at South Mountain on the 13th of September, and at Antietam on the 17th, on both of which occasions the officers and men distinguished themselves for coolness and bravery. In the Antietam fight the regiment lost nearly one fifth of its whole number of men engaged, and was highly complimented by Gen. Burnside. At the battle of Fredericksburg the Sixth behaved with great gallantry, and lost seventy-five men, killed and wounded, or nearly one third of the whole number engaged.

About the first of April, 1863, the Sixth went to Kentucky, under Gen. Burnside, and the last of May joined Gen. Grant in his operations on Vicksburg. Early in the winter the men very generally reënlisted for another term of three years, or during the war, and on the 30th of January, 1864, those who had reënlisted came home on a thirty days' furlough. In March the regiment returned to the scene of war and went into Camp at Annapolis, and subsequently joined the army of the Potomac, under Gen. Grant, and was actively engaged all summer, participating in many battles and skirmishes. From December until the surrender of that place, on the 2d of April, 1865, the Sixth was engaged in the siege of Petersburg. Thence it went in pursuit of Gen. Lee and his army, and after the surrender on the 9th, the war being virtually at an end, the regiment went into camp at Alexandria, where it remained until the 17th of July, when it was mustered out and returned home.

During its term of service the Sixth was in the following battles: Camden, N. C., Second Bull Run, Chantilly, South Mountain, Antietam, Fredericksburg, Siege of Vicksburg, Jackson, Wilderness, Spottsylvania Court House, 12th and 18th of May, 1864, North Anna River, Tolopotomy Creek, Bethesda Church, Cold Harbor, Petersburg, June 16th, 17th and 18th, 1864, Weldon Railroad, Poplar Spring Church, Hatcher's Run, Petersburg, April 2, 1865.

No regiment from this or any other State won a prouder name, or made a more honorable record than the New-Hampshire Sixth.

Surgeon SHERMAN COOPER,

Commissioned Assistant Surgeon of the 6th Reg't, Oct. 17, 1861. Promoted to Surgeon March 20, 1863. On arriving at Hatteras he was placed in charge of the hospital ship of Burnside's Expedition, which position he held until after the taking of Roanoke Island, in February, 1862, when the hospital was transferred to land, and he still remained in charge until March, when he went with his regiment to Roanoke Island. In May he was detailed to take charge of the Post Hospital at Roanoke Island, where he remained until July, when he joined his regiment at Newburn, N. C.

They joined Pope's Campaign, through which he was the only medical officer in the regiment. After the battle of Antietam he was detailed to take charge of a hospital at Weaverton, Md., containing fifteen hundred men, where he remained a month and until the men were returned to their regiments, sent to convalescent camp, or otherwise disposed of. From there he rode alone, on horseback, through the rebel country, a distance of sixty miles, to Washington, and afterward joined his regiment at Falmouth, Va., the 1st of November, where he remained until after the battle of Fredericksburg, on the 13th of December. He was then detailed as medical officer in charge of six batteries of artillery, called the Artillery Brigade, under Gen. Hunt, and was on the field with them seven days, at Fredericksburg. He remained with them through the winter. In the spring of 1863 he joined his regiment and went with it to Newport News, thence to Kentucky, and thence to Vicksburg. After the taking of that place the regiment was in the siege of Jackson, during which Dr. Cooper had charge of his brigade on the field, and was under fire eight consecutive days. After the taking of Jackson, the Ninth Army Corps, to which his regiment was attached returned to the Yazoo River, and he was placed in charge of the second division hospital of that corps, and in ten days after was ordered to the general superintendence of all the hospitals in the Ninth Corps. In about two weeks he was ordered by Gen. Parks to Vicksburg to charter boats and fit them for hospitals, and take the sick and wounded of the corps to Cincinnati. He placed the men in hospital, turned over the property and remained in Cincinnati about two weeks, waiting for the troops to come up. Joined the Corps at Nicholasville, Ky., and was Surgeon-in-chief of the Second Division of the Ninth Army Corps. From there he went to Camp Nelson, Ky., and was appointed Post Surgeon, which place he held until the regiment came home on veteran furlough, in January, 1864. In March the regiment returned and rejoined the Ninth Army Corps, and Dr. Cooper was appointed Surgeon in charge of the field hospital of the Second Division, which he held one month, and was relieved at his own request and placed upon the Operating Staff, which position he held until his three years were out, in November, 1864. During the month of July he performed with his own hands every operation in the Second Division of the Ninth Army Corps. In the time that he was Assistant Surgeon he was upon the field in every battle in which his regiment was engaged. During the whole three years Dr. Cooper was blessed with good health, performed an immense amount of hard work, and rendered valuable service in whatever capacity he was placed. The surgeon in charge of the Ninth Army Corps, a regular army officer, wrote of him to a friend — "Dr. Cooper has been for a long time at our Second Division Hospital, and is one of our ablest and most accomplished surgeons." He resigned and was mustered out of the service Nov. 30, 1864, returned to Claremont the following February, and is now here in the practice of his profession. He is a son of Hon. Lemuel P. Cooper of Croydon, and brother-in-law of the late Col. Gardiner of the 14th Regiment.

WILLIAM H. HADLEY

Enlisted as a recruit, and was mustered into Co. G, 6th Reg't, Aug. 26, 1862. Discharged at Milldale, Miss., July 1, 1863. He enlisted from purely patriotic motives, when too old to be drafted, and proved a most faithful soldier. He is father of Charles L. Hadley.

CHARLES L. HADLEY

Enlisted and was mustered into Co. G, 6th Reg't, as a musician, Nov. 28, 1861. Discharged for disability, at Camp Nelson, Ky., Feb. 3, 1864. He enlisted again and was mustered into Co. A, Heavy Artillery, Aug. 30, 1864, served to the end of the war, and was mustered out Aug. 31, 1865. It is but justice to say that his disability was caused by arduous service in carrying wounded men from the field under fire during the second Bull Run battle. He was a brave soldier, and always faithful to his duty. He is a son of William H. Hadley of the 6th Reg't, and is now clerk in a wholesale mercantile establishment in Boston.

EDGAR T. REED

Enlisted as a recruit, and was mustered into Co. G, 6th Reg't, March 6, 1864. Wounded June 7th, and also July 27th, 1864. Transferred to the Veteran Reserve Corps, and was subsequently shot through the head and killed by a deserter while attempting to capture him. He was a son of Levi F. Reed of the 5th Regiment.

EDWARD E. STORY

Enlisted and was mustered into Co. B, 6th Reg't, Nov. 27, 1861; transferred to Co. G, Dec. 1, 1861, and appointed Corporal. In April, 1861, he enlisted under Capt. Austin for three months, and at Portsmouth reënlisted for three years. He came home on a furlough, was taken down with measles, could not return to be mustered with his regiment, and was discharged. At the time of his muster into the 6th Reg't his health was quite poor. He suffered much from exposure on the passage to Hatteras Inlet, was taken sick soon after he arrived there, and died of typhoid fever in hospital on the 4th of March, 1862. He was a bookbinder by trade; twenty-three years old; son of Francis B. and Olive G. Story; brother of Charles C. Story of the 6th Mass. Reg't, and half brother of David H. Grannis of the 3d New-Hampshire Regiment.

RUSSELL TYLER

Enlisted and was mustered into Co. G, 6th Reg't, Dec. 3, 1861, when seventeen years old. Reënlisted Dec. 21, 1863. Wounded May 12, 1864, and again at Weldon Railroad, June 22, 1864. Promoted to First Lieutenant March 4, 1865, for his coolness and bravery in action. He was wounded again April 2, 1865, and was mustered out July 17, 1865. He is a son of Charles Tyler, formerly of this town, but now living at Cornish Flat, and was among the best soldiers who went from Claremont. While Sergeant he served on the color guard, one of the most dangerous and arduous places in the regiment. In February, 1862, he was left at Annapolis, sick with measles. When convalescent he was sent to the front to assist in McClellan's Peninsular Campaign, joined a Massachusetts regiment, and then the 2d New-Hampshire. He was in four battles before he rejoined his own regiment, which in the time had been in but one.

SEVENTH REGIMENT.

All the preceding regiments had been enlisted and equipped by the State Government. On the 2d of September, 1861, Joseph C. Abbott, of Manchester, late Adjutant-General of the State, received authority from the War Department to raise a regiment of Infantry in the State of New-Hampshire. This was at a time when the State was engaged in enlisting and getting ready for the field four regiments of infantry, a battery, three companies of sharp-shooters, and a battalion of cavalry. The State extended to this regiment the ten dollars bounty that had been offered to the men enlisting in the other corps. The regiment was enlisted and organized under the direction of Gen. Abbott, having its rendezvous at Manchester. Haldimand S. Putnam, a graduate of West Point, Lieutenant in the United States Topographical Engineers, a most accomplished young officer, and son of Hon. John L. Putnam of Cornish, was appointed Colonel; Joseph C. Abbott of Manchester, Lieut. Colonel, and Daniel Smith of Dover, Major. The muster of the regiment was completed on the 14th of December. On the 14th of January, 1862, it left the State, and went into barracks in New-York, where it remained about a month, when it departed for the Dry Tortugas, where it remained three months guarding government stores, Col. Putnam being commander of the post. From here the regiment was removed to Beaufort, where it remained until the 1st of September, when it was ordered to St. Augustine, Florida. Up to this time it had suffered severe losses from disease incident to the change of climate and other causes. In May, 1863, the regiment went to Fernandina, thence in June to Hilton Head, and joined an expedition against Charleston.

. The memorable assault on Fort Wagner took place on the 18th of July. The Seventh Regiment numbered but four hundred and eighty officers and men fit for duty. During the battle, which lasted an hour and a half, and proved a disaster rather than a success, the loss to the regiment in killed, wounded and missing, was two hundred and eighteen. Col. Putnam was among the killed, and Everett W. Nelson of Claremont, a brave soldier, was mortally wounded, taken prisoner, and died of his wounds at Charleston, S. C., six days after the battle. After this assault a long and arduous siege commenced, and the Seventh Regiment was employed in the trenches. On the 7th of September another assault upon Fort Wagner had been determined upon, when it was found that the Fort had been evacuated. On the 20th of December the regiment moved to St. Helena Island, opposite Hilton Head, where it remained until the 14th of February, 1864, when it joined Gen. Seymour in his campaign into Florida, and on the 20th was engaged in a battle near Olustee, and lost two hundred and nine men in killed and wounded. On the 17th of April it returned to Fortress Monroe, and joined the army of the James, under Gen. Butler, and was engaged in the final advance on Richmond. It was actively engaged throughout the whole campaign and was in many battles. The Seventh was engaged in a second trial on Fort Fisher, January 13, 1865, and subsequently garrisoned Wilmington, N. C. Early in June it was sent to Goldsborough, N. C., where it remained until ordered to be discharged. The regiment returned to Concord on the 30th of July, where it was handsomely received by state officials and the people, and the men mustered out of service.

WILLIAM DOOLEY

Enlisted and was mustered into Co. II, 7th Reg't, Dec. 14, 1861. Discharged for disability July 20, 1862.

MOSES GARFIELD

Enlisted and was mustered into Co. II, 7th Reg't, Dec. 14, 1861. Reënlisted for a second term of three years, or during the war, Feb. 29, 1864. Died of disease at Goldsborough, N. C., June 29, 1865.

JOHN W. HAMMOND

Enlisted and was mustered into Co. II, 7th Reg't, Dec. 14, 1861. Discharged for disability, at Fort Jefferson, Fla., July 20, 1862. Enlisted into the Veteran Reserve Corps, Jan. 31, 1865, served to the end of the war, and was mustered out Nov. 7, 1865.

J. FISHER LAWRENCE

Enlisted and was mustered into Co. II, 7th Reg't, as a musician, Dec. 14, 1861. Died of disease at Port Royal, Aug. 8, 1862. He left a wife and children.

EDWIN MARSTON

Enlisted and was mustered into Co. II, 7th Reg't, Dec. 14, 1861. Discharged for disability July 20, 1862.

AZRO J. MANN

Enlisted and was mustered into Co. II, 7th Reg't, Dec. 14, 1861. Wounded at Chattanooga,

Aug. 30, 1863. Discharged on account of wounds, at Beaufort, S. C., July 31, 1864.

EVERETT W. NELSON

Enlisted under Capt. Austin for three months, in April, 1861; went to Portsmouth, but declined to reënlist for three years, and was sent to Fort Constitution, where he served out his term of enlistment. Enlisted and was mustered into Co. H, 7th Reg't, Dec. 14, 1861. Wounded and taken prisoner at Fort Wagner, July 18, 1863; was carried to Charleston, S. C., and died of his wounds on the 24th of the same month. He was born at Wayne, Me., in 1830, came to Claremont in 1851, and worked at his trade as a shoemaker, until he enlisted. Fort Wagner was the first battle in which his regiment was engaged. He left a widow and two young children. He was a good soldier and a worthy man.

Lieutenant MANSEL OTIS

Enlisted and was mustered into Co. A, 7th Reg't, Oct. 29, 1861. Promoted to Sergeant. Promoted to Second Lieutenant Jan. 1, 1864. On the breaking out of the rebellion, in April, 1861, he enlisted in a Massachusetts three months regiment, and at the expiration of his term returned to Claremont.

WILLARD C. SEVERANCE

Enlisted as a recruit, and was mustered into Co. H, 7th Reg't, Dec. 18, 1863. Appointed Corporal June 2, 1865. Mustered out July 20, 1865.

JESSE SPARLING

Enlisted and was mustered into Co. H, 7th Reg't, Dec. 14, 1861. Discharged for disability in March, 1862. When the regiment left New-York he was sick, and never rejoined it.

Sergeant CHESTER M. SPRAGUE

Enlisted as a recruit, and was mustered into Co. H, 7th Reg't, Sept. 5, 1862. Appointed Corporal. Promoted to Sergeant Dec. 28, 1864. Wounded Jan. 19, 1865. Mustered out July 17, 1865. He was a brave soldier.

ANDREW WALKER

Enlisted and was mustered into Co. H, 7th Reg't, Dec. 14, 1861. Discharged Sept. 25, 1862. Father of George H. Walker of the same company.

AUGUSTUS E. WOODBURY

Enlisted as a recruit, and was mustered into Co. H, 7th Reg't, Dec. 18, 1863. Wounded and captured at Olustee, Fla., Feb. 10, 1864. Died of disease at Andersonville, Ga., June 23, 1864. He was but seventeen years old when he enlisted. Son of Franklin Woodbury of Claremont.

GEORGE H. WALKER

Enlisted and was mustered into Co. H, 7th Reg't, Dec. 14, 1861. Wounded Feb. 20, 1864. Served to the end of his term, and was mustered out Dec. 22, 1864. He is a son of Andrew Walker.

HARVEY WARD

Enlisted and was mustered into Co. A, 7th Reg't, Oct. 29, 1861. Discharged for disability July 20, 1862.

EIGHTH REGIMENT.

This regiment was organized at Manchester in the fall of 1861. It was mostly composed of men belonging in the central portion of the State. The bounty was the same as that paid to the men of the preceding regiments. The field officers were Hawkes. Fearing, Jr., of Manchester, Colonel; Oliver W. Lull of Milford, Lieut. Colonel, and Morrill W. Smith of Concord, Major. The muster of this regiment was completed on the 23d of December, 1861, and it left the State on the 24th of January, 1862. As no Claremont men were in this regiment, a detailed account of its operations is not important to this history. It joined General Butler's expedition, and was assigned to General Phelps' brigade. It passed the summer of 1862 near New-Orleans. Subsequently it was at the siege of Port Hudson and in other engagements, showed great bravery, was highly commended by commanding generals, and suffered severely in several battles. Those men of the regiment who did not reënlist returned home under command of Col. Fearing early in January, 1865, and were mustered out of service, while those who had reenlisted, together with the recruits whose term of service had not expired, were formed into a veteran battalion and remained in service until the 9th of November, 1865, when they returned to Concord and were discharged.

NINTH REGIMENT.

This regiment was organized in the summer of 1862, its muster being completed on the 23d of August. The State offered to each man who would enlist to fill regiments already in the field, a bounty of sixty dollars, and to those enlisting to form new regiments a bounty of fifty dollars. The field officers were Enoch Q. Fellows of Sandwich, Colonel; Herbert B. Titus of Chesterfield, Lieut. Colonel, and George W. Everett of New-London, Major. Col. Fellows was Adjutant of the First and Colonel of the Third, which latter position he resigned; and Lieut. Colonel Titus was promoted from a Lieutenancy in the Second regiment.

The Ninth left the State on the 25th of August, and joined McClellan's army of the Potomac, and on the 14th of September had its first experience under fire at the battle of South Mountain, where twenty-five of its men were wounded, two of whom subsequently died of their wounds. On the 17th, three days after, this regiment was in the battle at

Antietam, and behaved nobly. It lost in this engagement ten killed and eighty wounded. Among the latter were Lieut. Col. Titus and two Captains. At the battle of Fredericksburg, on the 13th of December, the Ninth fought bravely, and lost four men killed and eighty-two wounded. In the spring of 1863, the Ninth went with Gen. Burnside to Tennessee, and was engaged in performing provost and guard duty. Thence it went to Mississippi and participated in the battle near Jackson on the 12th and 13th of July. Subsequently it was transferred to Kentucky and assigned to provost duty at Paris. It was also in the battle of the Wilderness in May 1864. At Spottsylvania it had forty-two men killed, ninety-four wounded, and seventy were missing. It was in the battle of Cold Harbor, and subsequently spent two months in the trenches before Petersburg, participating in the battle of the "Mine," on the 30th of July, and was the first regiment to plant its colors on the ruined works. In this conflict the loss to the regiment in killed and wounded was heavy—nearly one half of its number engaged. On the 30th of September it was engaged in the battle of Poplar Grove Church, and did good service. Lieut. Wm. D. Rice of Claremont is supposed to have been killed in this battle. The last of November it went into camp and passed a quiet winter. In the battles the following April, which sealed the fate of the Confederacy, the Ninth was not engaged, being a part of the force left to hold the lines in front of Petersburg. It was detailed, with two other regiments, to guard Ewell's army of eight thousand men, which was captured on the 6th of April.

On the 23d of May the regiment participated in the grand review of the army at Washington, after which the recruits in this were transferred to the Sixth regiment, and on the 10th of June, under command of Col. Titus, the Ninth left for home, and was mustered out of the service on the 14th, leaving an honorable record.

JAMES P. BASCOM

Enlisted and was mustered into Co. G, 9th Reg't, August 13, 1862. He was in three engagements with his regiment, the last of which was the battle of Fredericksburg, Va., Dec. 13, 1862. Soon after this battle he was taken sick with typhoid fever, and died in the regimental hospital, at Falmouth, Va., on the 25th of December, 1862. He was the third son of Elisha Bascom of Claremont, and brother of Wallace Bascom of the 2d Mass. regiment, who was killed in the battle of Gettysburg.

In speaking of James P. Bascom, the commanding officer of his company, in a letter to his father informing him of the death of his son, wrote — "He was always prompt whenever called upon; respectful both to men and officers; always ready in time of danger to do his part to extricate us out of it." He was buried near Falmouth, but his remains were subsequently brought home and buried by those of the other members of his family. His funeral was attended at the Methodist church, Rev. Mr. Hartwell preaching the sermon. At the time of his death he was about twenty-two years old. He was a worthy young man.

AMOS F. BRADFORD

Enlisted and was mustered into Co. G, 9th Reg't, Aug. 13, 1862. Died of diphtheria, at Paris, Ky., Nov. 10, 1863, and was buried there. He participated in the battles of Antietam and South Mountain. His brother, Caleb M. D. Bradford of Charlestown, was in the same company. Another brother, Hosea B. Bradford, enlisted at Topeka, Kansas, and died of fever at Leavenworth City, Jan. 13, 1864. Another, David H. Bradford, enlisted in Colorado, in September 1862, was wounded at the battle of Little Blue River, in October, 1864, and died of his wounds three weeks afterward. These four were sons of the late Thomas Bradford of Claremont.

GEORGE W. CURRIER

Enlisted and was mustered into Co. K, 9th Reg't, Aug. 15, 1862. Discharged for disability at Falmouth, Va., Feb. 29, 1863, came home in a very feeble state, and soon after died of chronic diarrhea.

Sergeant NEWELL T. DUTTON

Enlisted and was mustered into Co. E, 9th Reg't, Aug. 6, 1862. Promoted to Sergeant Major Feb. 1, 1865. He served faithfully to the end of the war, was mustered out with his regiment, came home, and is now pursuing a course of study at Brown University. He is a son of Aaron Dutton of Claremont, and a brother of Lewis H. Dutton, of the 3d Vermont regiment. His bravery as a soldier was never called in question.

NATHAN HARRIS

Enlisted and was mustered into Co. G, 9th Reg't, Aug. 13, 1862. Discharged for disability Aug. 19, 1863. He is a farmer by occupation, and before his enlistment lived with the late Harvey Tolles of Claremont.

CHARLES R. JACKSON

Enlisted from the town of Unity, and was mustered into Co. K, 9th Reg't, in August, 1862. He was in several battles, among them South Mountain, Sharpsburg, Antietam and Jackson, escaping unhurt. He fell sick, and after remaining in hospital eight months, came home on a furlough — his wife then living in Claremont — and died on the 3d of December, 1863. His funeral took place at the Methodist church, and his remains were buried, agreeably to his request, in the old grave-yard, by those of his father and other members of his family. He was born in Claremont in 1838, and was a son of the late Joseph Jackson.

GEORGE W. KENERSON

Enlisted and was mustered into Co. G, 9th Reg't, Aug. 13, 1862. Transferred to Veteran Reserve Corps Jan. 15, 1864. Mustered out June 30, 1865.

CHARLES B. MARVIN

Enlisted and was mustered into Co. G, 9th Reg't, Aug. 19, 1862. Killed at the battle of Antietam, Sept. 17, 1862, and buried upon the field. His remains were subsequently brought to Westminster, Vt., and buried by the side of those of his father. He was eighteen years old at the time of his death, and though but a short time in the army, showed himself a brave soldier. He was a son of the late Giles P. Marvin, and brother of Giles P. Marvin, of the First Connecticut Cavalry.

CHARLES H. MURPHY

Enlisted and was mustered into Co. G, 9th Reg't, Aug. 14, 1862. Wounded May 18, 1864. Mustered out June 10, 1865.

CHARLES B. MANN

Enlisted and was mustered into Co. G, 9th Reg't, Aug. 13, 1862. Wounded May 31, 1864, at Cold Harbor. Transferred to Veteran Reserve Corps, May 1, 1865. Mustered out July 1, 1865.

FRANKLIN G. NEVERS

Enlisted and was mustered into Co. G, 9th Reg't, Aug. 13, 1862. Captured Aug. 30, 1864. Paroled March 2, 1865. Mustered out June 2, 1865.

Lieutenant WILLIAM DANFORD RICE

Enlisted as a private, and was mustered into Co. G, 9th Reg't, Aug. 13, 1862, and the same day appointed Sergeant. At the battles of South Mountain, on the 14th, and Antietam on the 17th, of September, he behaved with such coolness, vigilance and efficiency as to attract the notice of his officers and win their hearty commendation, and gained in a marked degree the confidence of the men. At the battle of Fredericksburg, Dec. 13, 1862, Captain, afterward Lieut. Colonel Whitfield,- although on account of wounds received in the battle of Antietam, was not in the fight, says he was informed by officers of the regiment that Sergeant Rice particularly distinguished himself. In the temporary absence of the only commissioned officer of the company he assumed command and directed its movements with the coolness and skill of a veteran officer. Soon he was promoted to Orderly Sergeant, which position he filled very acceptably until Jan. 1, 1864, when he was again promoted to Second Lieutenant. He was severely wounded in the left hand in the battle of the Wilderness, May 12, 1864. Being unfit for duty he was for a few weeks home on a furlough, and then returned to Convalescent Camp, Annapolis, Md., where, when he had recovered sufficiently, he was placed upon a Court Marshal, which position he occupied several weeks, and then returned to his regiment. While at Annapolis he was offered the charge of all the rebel prisoners at Elmira, N. Y., but declined it, feeling that he was most needed with his regiment. After the battle of Poplar

Grove Church, Sept. 30, 1864, where Lieut. Rice was acting Adjutant of his regiment, and was also the only commissioned officer of his company, he was missing. Our forces were obliged to retreat, and while doing so a corporal of his company saw Lieut. Rice fall upon his face, apparently killed or mortally wounded. This is the last authentic account of him. If not killed he fell into the hands of the enemy and died a prisoner. He was respected and beloved by every officer and man in his regiment. Capt. Case, of Co. G, wrote Lieut. Rice's father, soon after he was missing—"It is useless for me to add any thing more in regard to your son. He was a noble-hearted young man, actuated by the most generous and patriotic motives, and whether living or dead his name and the record which he left with his regiment and all who knew him, was such as any one might envy; and if he has fallen it was nobly doing his whole duty, like a man fighting in a just and holy cause." One of the privates in his company wrote home to a friend—"He was loved by every man in his command, and the officers throughout the regiment. There was no braver officer in the whole regiment than Lieut. William D. Rice. He did not fear the enemy one mite. He was always at the post of duty. We must look to the Great Being above us, who doeth all things well, for his safety. The Company deeply feel the loss of so good and brave a man.". Lieut. Col. Whitfield writes—"I can not close without bearing further evidence to the worth of one who has 'given the last full measure of his devotion.' Honest, brave and conscientious in the discharge of his duty, his manliness yet asserted itself in all his acts. He bent no supple knee 'that thrift might follow fawning,' but yet was second to none in respect for, and subordination to, commands of his superior officers. As a non-commissioned officer he was strictly impartial in all his dealings with the men, and though often called upon to perform most disagreeable duties, performed them in such a manner as to gain the respect of all. No soldier has a more thankless office than an Orderly Sergeant, and of none did I ever hear less complaint than was made of him. Blessed with excellent health he was always at his post, and with energies never flagging omitted no jot or tittle of the work laid out for him to do. Of his moral character I need not speak. It is too well known for any words of mine to add to or detract from. Strictly temperate he exacted of others the abstinence that in himself was a virtue, never a necessity. The influence of judicious home training and the loving care of a christian mother seemed to have left their impress too deeply for all the varied excitements and demoralizing tendencies of camp life to efface." Lieut. Rice was the youngest son of Danford Rice of West Claremont. He was born here Nov. 21, 1843, entered Kimball Union Academy, Meriden, at the age of fifteen years, and continued there several terms. He had been recommended by the most influential men in the State for an appointment to West Point Military Academy whenever one should be made from this Congressional District. The loss of such young men leads us to consider most seriously the cost of the late war.

JOHN H. RUGG

Enlisted and was mustered into Co. G, 9th Reg't, Aug. 19, 1861. Discharged June 26, 1863. Enlisted into the Veteran Reserve Corps, Feb. 18, 1864.

GEORGE W. RUSSELL

Enlisted and was mustered into Co. G, 9th Reg't, Aug. 13, 1862. His regiment was in the battle of Antietam, Sept. 17, 1862. During the battle his Colonel, Titus, discovered that a rebel sharpshooter, concealed behind a large tree, was picking off our men, and ordered Capt. Whitfield to detail a number of his men to capture or kill the rebel. Mr. Russell was one of the number called to this duty, and while attempting to carry out the Colonel's order received a severe wound from a minnie ball, in the abdomen. When shot he remarked to a comrade near him,—"I am shot. He has fixed me." He went alone to the rear, but was carried to the regimental hospital, where he died at three o'clock next morning. He was buried by his fellow-soldiers. Mr. Russell was thirty years old at the time of his death; was a native of Sutton, this State; a carpenter by trade; a worthy man and a good soldier, who shirked no duty. He left a widow and two small children to mourn his death.

LYMAN N. SARGENT

Enlisted and was mustered into Co. G, 9th Reg't, Aug. 13, 1862. He was wounded in the right ankle at the battle of Cold Harbor, May 31, 1864, by a minnie ball. His foot was amputated just above the ankle joint, the same day, upon the field. He was discharged by special order, July 1, 1865, and came home. His leg had not healed, gangrene set in, and a second amputation, below the knee, was performed by Dr. Nathaniel Tolles of Claremont, on the 7th of October, 1865. He participated in the battles of South Mountain, Antietam, Fredericksburg, the Wilderness, Spottsylvania and Cold Harbor, and was a faithful soldier.

HARVEY H. SARGENT

Enlisted and was mustered into Co. G, 9th Reg't, Aug. 13, 1862. Transferred to Veteran Reserve Corps Jan. 16, 1864. Mustered out July 13, 1865. He is a son of Winthrop Sargent of Claremont, and now lives in Lawrence, Mass.

AI R. SHORT

Enlisted and was mustered into Co. G, 9th Reg't, Aug. 13, 1862. Discharged for disability Oct. 30, 1862. Enlisted and was mustered into Co. A, Heavy Artillery, Aug. 31, 1864. Mustered out Aug. 31, 1865.

SAMUEL C. TOWNE

Enlisted and was mustered into Co. G, 9th Reg't, Aug. 13, 1862. Served until the end of the war, and was mustered out June 10, 1865. He is a brother of Matthew T. Towne of the 5th Reg't, and son of David Towne of Claremont.

Corporal LORENZO M. UPHAM

Enlisted and was mustered into Co. G, 9th Reg't, Aug. 13, 1862, and appointed Corporal. He was accidentally wounded in the hand by the discharge of his own gun, during the battle of Antietam, Sept. 17, 1862. Discharged on account of wound, Oct. 30, 1862.

Sergeant GEORGE L. WAKEFIELD

Enlisted and was mustered into Co. G, 9th Reg't, Aug. 13, 1862. Appointed Corporal. Wounded in right arm and missing Sept. 30, 1864. Gained from missing. Promoted to Sergeant May 1, 1865. Mustered out June 10, 1865. Although not more than seventeen years old when he entered into the army, he proved a good soldier. He is a son of the late Harvey M. Wakefield of the 5th Reg't.

TENTH REGIMENT.

In July, 1862, the President issued a call for three hundred thousand three years troops, which was soon followed by a call for the same number of nine months volunteers, to meet what seemed to be an urgent necessity. These calls were enthusiastically responded to by New-Hampshire. The Tenth Regiment was enlisted under the first call, and went into camp at Manchester. Its muster was completed on the 5th of September, and the regiment left the State for the seat of war on the 22d. The field officers were Michael T. Donohoe of Manchester, Colonel, who was promoted from Captain in the Third, John Coughlin of Manchester, Lieut. Colonel, and Jesse F. Angell of Manchester, Major. Claremont furnished but three men for this regiment.

The Tenth joined the Army of the Potomac, sharing its fortunes and participating in its battles. It was at the battle of Fredericksburg, and lost three officers wounded, and fifty men killed and wounded. It was also in the battle of Cold Harbor, and remained at the front from the 3d to the 12th of June, 1864, more or less of its men being killed and wounded every day. On the 28th of September, it bore a conspicuous part in the taking of Fort Harrison, losing, out of less than two hundred officers and men who went into the fight, thirty-four killed and wounded. On the 25th of October, in a charge upon the rebels near Fair Oaks, the regiment suffered severely. Only two of the ten officers escaped, and seventy-four men were either killed, wounded, or taken prisoners. Nearly all the men who were captured died in the prison pen at Salisbury, N. C. At the final triumphant advance on Richmond, the Tenth was among the first to enter the city. On the 25th of June, 1865, in company with the Twelfth and Thirteenth regiments, forming a brigade, under command of Brevet Brigadier General M. T. Donohoe, it returned to Concord and was mustered out, having earned its share of the glory of putting down the rebellion.

Corporal ALFRED W. BURRILL

Enlisted and was mustered into Co. A, 10th Reg't, Aug. 20, 1862. Promoted to Corporal. Detailed as Brigade Mail Carrier at Suffolk, Va., in March, 1863. Returned to regiment in September, 1864. Wounded at the battle of Fort Harrison, Va., Sept. 29, 1864. Mustered out with his regiment May 25, 1865. He is a son of Alfred Burrill of Claremont, and brother of Charles F. Burrill of the 5th Reg't, who was killed at the battle of Gettysburg.

PATRICK O'CONNELL

Enlisted and was mustered into Co. F, 10th Reg't, Sept. 1, 1862. Transferred to Veteran Reserve Corps Aug. 20, 1863. Discharged for disability. Died at Philadelphia, Sept. 3, 1864.

JOHN HERRIN

Enlisted as a recruit, and was mustered into Co. F, 10th Reg't, Aug. 24, 1864. Captured at Fair Oaks, Oct. 27, 1864. Exchanged March 23, 1865. Transferred to 2d regiment June 21, 1865. Mustered out July 7, 1865.

ELEVENTH REGIMENT.

This regiment was enlisted in August, 1862, and went into Camp at Concord. The field officers were Walter Harriman of Warner, Colonel; Moses A. Collins of Exeter, Lieut. Colonel, and Evarts W. Farr of Littleton, formerly Captain in the Second, Major. The regiment left Concord on the 11th of September and joined the army of the Potomac on the 3d of October. It was in the battle of Fredericksburg on the 13th of December, and behaved so well as to receive the commendation of the commanding General. It suffered the loss of fourteen killed, fifty-six wounded, and twenty-four missing. A few of the latter, however, returned to the regiment.

In March, 1863, the regiment went to Kentucky, and was for about a year in that State, Tennessee and Missouri, and was engaged in the Mississippi campaign, and the siege of Knoxville in November, 1863. In May, 1864, it was in the battle of the Wilderness, where Col. Harriman was taken prisoner, and Lieut. Col. Collins was killed. It was also engaged, from the 12th to the 18th of May, in the battle at Spottsylvania Court House, where our army captured the rebel General Bushrod Johnson, and five thousand of his men. It participated in the battle of Cold Harbor on the 3d of June. In the months of June and July the Eleventh was in the trenches before Petersburg, and took an active part in the battle of the "Mine," on the 30th of July, losing heavily. Its colors were twice lost and twice retaken, and finally were torn in two, the enemy retaining half, while the remainder was saved with the regiment. It was in the battle of Poplar Grove Church and Pegram's Farm, on the 30th September; Hatcher's Run, 27th of October, and was in the works in front of Petersburg from the 29th of November, 1864, until the 2d of April, 1865. It was engaged in the final battles which resulted in the extinguishment of the rebellion, and was in the grand review at Washington, on the 23d and 24th of May. The Eleventh returned to Concord on the 7th of June, had a warm reception, and was mustered out on the 10th, leaving a proud record.

Sergeant GEORGE E. ROWELL

Enlisted and was mustered into Co. H, 11th Reg't, Sept. 2, 1862. Promoted to Sergeant.

Died of disease at Baltimore, Md., April 10, 1864. He was a good soldier and a worthy young man. Was a brother of Henry L. Rowell of the 5th Regiment, and son of the late James E. Rowell of Claremont.

TWELFTH REGIMENT.

This regiment was mostly enlisted in Belknap County, and went into camp at Concord on the 3d of September, 1862. The field officers were Joseph H. Potter, a native of Concord, and a graduate of West Point, Colonel; John F. Marsh of Nashua, Lieut. Colonel, and George D. Savage of Alton, Major. No Claremont men were in the original organization of this regiment.

The Twelfth left Concord on the 27th of September, and joined the army of the Potomac, for the most part sharing its battles and fortunes during its term of service. It formed a part of the army that entered Richmond, on the morning of the 3d of April, 1865 ; was the first to take possession of Jefferson Davis' mansion, and helped to save the city from total destruction by the fire kindled by rebel hands. In June, the Twelfth, brigaded with the Tenth and Thirteenth New-Hampshire Regiments, under command of Brigadier General M. T. Donohoe, returned to Concord, was handsomely received and cordially welcomed by the people and State officials, and mustered out on the 3d of July, leaving a record of which no member need be ashamed.

THIRTEENTH REGIMENT.

This regiment was enlisted in August and September, 1862, and went into camp at Concord the last part of September. It contained but one man from Claremont. The field officers were Aaron F. Stevens of Nashua, who was Major of the First Regiment, Colonel; George Bowers of Nashua, who served in the Mexican war, Lieut. Colonel, and Jacob Storer of Portsmouth, Major. The regiment left the State on the 6th of October, and joined the army of the Potomac. Its history, while in the field, is not dissimilar to that of the others which were connected with the army during the three years preceding the surrender of the rebel armies. It distinguished itself for coolness and bravery in many battles, and suffered severely in killed and wounded in most of them. In November, 1864, authority was given the regiment, by the General commanding the army, to place upon its national colors the names and dates of the following engagements, in which it had borne an honorable part: Fredericksburg, December 13, 1862; Siege of Suffolk, April and May, 1863; Walthal Road, May 7, 1864; Swift Creek, May 9, 1864; Kingsland Creek, May 12 and 13, 1864; Drury's Bluff, May 14 and 16, 1864; Cold Harbor, June 1 and 3, 1864; Battery 5, Petersburg, June 15, 1864; Battery Harrison, September 29 and 30, 1864.

The colors of the Thirteenth were the first carried into the city of Richmond, on the 3d of April, 1865. It returned to Concord as a part of the Brigade with the Tenth and Twelfth Regiments, under Gen. Donohoe, in June, 1865, and was mustered out on the 1st of July.

HENRY V. FREEMAN

Enlisted and was mustered into Co. E, 13th Reg't, Sept. 26, 1862. Served to the end of the war, was mustered out June 9, 1865, and returned to his home in Claremont. He was the only man in that regiment from Claremont.

FOURTEENTH REGIMENT.

This regiment was recruited in the months of August and September, 1862. It went into camp at Concord, and its muster was completed on the 24th of September. The field officers were Robert Wilson of Keene, Colonel; Tileston A. Barker of Westmoreland, promoted from Captain of the Second, Lieut. Colonel, and Samuel A. Duncan of Plainfield, Major. Claremont furnished a number of men for this regiment, which makes a more particular account of its movements and operations important to this history.

The Fourteenth left Concord for Washington the fore part of the month of October, 1862, and spent the winter doing guard and picket duty near that city. From April, 1863, to February, 1864, it did provost duty in Washington, when it was ordered to the Department of the Gulf, and arrived at New-Orleans on the 12th of April. In September, 1863, Major Duncan resigned, and Alexander Gardiner of Claremont was promoted from Adjutant to fill his place. On the 6th of June, 1864, the regiment moved from the defenses of New-Orleans to Morganzia, near the mouth of Red River, and joined the corps of Gen. Birge, where it remained in camp until the 3d of July, when it moved to the Shenandoah Valley and joined Sheridan's army at Berryville, on the 18th of August. In September, Col. Wilson having resigned, Major Gardiner was commissioned Colonel.

On the 19th of September occurred the battle near Winchester. About eleven o'clock an advance was ordered against the enemy's position, the Fourteenth being on the right of the front line. The advance was so impetuous, bringing our troops close upon a rebel battery, that they could not hold the ground. In falling back the regiment sustained a heavy loss. Thirteen of the twenty officers and one hundred and thirty men, who went into the fight, were killed, wounded or prisoners. Only eight were taken prisoners, and some of these were wounded. Col. Gardiner was mortally wounded, and died on the 8th of October; Capt. William H. Chaffin, and Lieut. Henry S. Paull, both of Claremont, were killed and left upon the field in the hands of the enemy. In the afternoon, about four o'clock, another advance was ordered, which was so well planned and so impetuous that the rebels were driven beyond Winchester, and our troops took twenty-five hundred prisoners, beside nearly all their wounded, and five pieces of artillery, and of course recovered our own dead and wounded. On the 20th the army moved after the retreating rebels, and on the 22d was fought the battle of Fisher's Hill, the Fourteenth, under command of Capt. Tollman, behaving splendidly. On the 19th of October another battle occurred at Fisher's Hill with Early's army, in which this regiment was engaged. The fore part of the day the contest seemed against us, our men being driven from their position, but at three o'clock in the afternoon our forces rallied and drove the rebels in great confusion to Mount Jackson. Two thousand prisoners, forty-eight cannon, ambulances, wagons, and five thousand stand of arms fell into our hands. The Fourteenth lost eight killed, fifty-five wounded, and sixteen prisoners.

Early in January, 1865, the Fourteenth was moved to Savannah, where it remained until May, when it marched to Augusta and guarded Jefferson Davis, and the prisoners taken with him, to the steamer that carried them to Savannah. The regiment returned to Concord and was mustered out of service on the 26th of July, 1865.

The Governor and Council of this State, learning that the thirty-three officers and men of the Fourteenth Regiment, who were killed at the battle of Winchester, had been buried in one grave, with nothing to show their identity, and no mark other than enough to indicate the number buried, their names, and the regiment to which they belonged, immediately took measures to have a suitable monument erected on the spot. The monument was dedicated on the 9th of April, 1866. Inscribed upon it are the following Claremont names: Capt. W. H. Chaffin and Lieut. Henry S. Paull, killed; Col. A. Gardiner, mortally wounded.

JOHN BOWLER

Enlisted and was mustered into Co. I, 14th Reg't, Sept. 24, 1862. Discharged for disability, at Washington, July 9, 1863.

CHARLES S. BOWKER

Enlisted and was mustered into Co. I, 14th Reg't, Sept. 24, 1862. Mustered out with Reg't, July 26, 1865.

FRED. L. BARKER

Enlisted and was mustered into Co. I, 14th Reg't, Sept. 14, 1862. Served faithfully until the end of the war, and was mustered out with the Reg't, July 26, 1865.

Captain WILLIAM HENRY CHAFFIN

Was commissioned Captain of Co. I, 14th Reg't, Dec. 18, 1862. At the battle of Opequan Creek, near Winchester, Va., Sept. 19, 1864, which was the first pitched battle the regiment was in, he was acting Lieut. Colonel, and was one of the first men killed. He was a son of John Chaffin of Claremont; was born here in 1839; graduated at Kimball Union Academy, Meriden, N. H., in 1861, and entered Norwich, Vt., Military University the same year, where he remained until the Autumn of 1862, when he was employed to drill recruits in the 14th New-Hampshire Regiment, at Concord. The following is a concise account of his military career, by his Colonel, Robert Wilson, of the 14th Regiment:

"My first acquaintance with William H. Chaffin commenced in August, 1862, when he came to Concord as military instructor for a squad of recruits enlisted by S. M. Bugbee and others. He exhibited great zeal in disciplining the men under his charge. Before the regiment left Concord, Bugbee fell sick and Chaffin went to Washington in command of Co. I, but without any commission.

Early in December Bugbee resigned, and I recommended that Chaffin be appointed Captain, and the same month he received his commission. Capt. Chaffin was always distinguished for his good soldierly qualities; his steady observance of duty under all hardships and trials—and they were many and oftentimes vexatious. I never heard a word of complaint or grumbling from officers or men of Co. I against their Captain, either for severity of discipline, or injustice in the management of company affairs. He was one of my most reliable officers, and when directed from Head Quarters to detail an officer for a particular duty, requiring decided courage, a cool, clear head under high responsibilities, and a thorough determination to do the duty with which he should be intrusted, I often selected Chaffin for its performance. His care for the privates of his company was untiring, and he generally reported more men fit for duty than any other company of the same size.

"In the summer of 1863, Capt. Chaffin was sent, with a detachment of about sixty men to the front, near the Rappahannock, to return a body of convalescents to their several regiments. When near his destination a large army train, loaded with fixed ammunition, was attacked by one hundred and fifty or two hundred of Moseby's guerrillas, disguised as Union soldiers. Several of the drivers were killed, the harnesses cut, near two hundred mules run off, and some wagons plundered of loose articles, when Chaffin and his men came up at double quick, saved the train, dispersed the guerrillas, and recovered one hundred and thirty or one hundred and forty of the mules.

"During the voyage to New-Orleans, in March, 1864, we encountered a severe gale, lasting five days, and no person on the vessel expected to escape from going down; yet Chaffin was active and efficient in the preservation of good discipline and in exciting cheerfulness among the men.

"In a reconnoissance in force, made September 5, 1864, near Berryville, Va., by order of Gen. Sheridan, the skirmish line consisted of some troops from New-York which did not advance with alacrity and boldness sufficient to satisfy our commander, and I was directed to call for volunteers from my regiment to perform that duty. Capt. Chaffin immediately stepped forward and offered his services. His offer was accepted, and he proceeded at once to push the enemy vigorously. The service was one of great danger, but there was no further complaint from our General in command of lack of energy and daring in the skirmishers. I resigned, and on the evening of Sept.

7, 1864, received my discharge, and was no longer in command. Twelve days afterward the battle of Opequan Creek occurred, and poor Chaffin, with many other brave men and officers, gave their lives for their country." His body fell into the hands of the enemy, but was afterward recovered and buried by his men. Soon after his death his father died, and the funeral sermon of both, at the same time, was preached at the Congregational Church, by Rev. E. W. Clark. He left a mother, one brother, and many friends to mourn his early death.

JOSEPH A. DICKEY

Enlisted and was mustered into Co. I, 14th Reg't, Oct. 6, 1862. Mustered out with the Reg't July 26, 1865.

Sergeant CHARLES E. FOSTER

Enlisted and was mustered into Co. I, 14th Reg't, Oct. 6, 1862. Promoted to Sergeant. Transferred to Veteran Reserve Corps Dec. 27, 1864. Mustered out June 26, 1865. He is a son of Rev. Mr. Foster, lately settled at Acworth, and a worthy man.

Colonel ALEXANDER GARDINER

Was appointed Adjutant of the 14th Reg't Sept. 20, 1862. Promoted to Major Sept. 12, 1863.

Promoted to Colonel Sept. 12, 1864. Mortally wounded in the battle of Opequan Creek, near Winchester, Va., Sept. 19, 1864, and died of his wounds Oct. 8, 1864. He remained five hours in the hands of the enemy, when our troops regained the ground and recovered the dead and wounded. Robert Wilson of Keene, who went out as Colonel of this regiment, and remained in command of it until Sept. 7, 1864, writes of Col. Gardiner—"The Adjutant was sworn in and assumed the duties of his office. The books were opened and business commenced systematically. Gardiner was indefatigable, and rendered me great assistance in the arduous details of organizing and disciplining the regiment. After the Fourteenth was ordered to Washington, in April, 1863, the duties of Adjutant became much more onerous, as the details for guard and police duty were so large as often to require every able-bodied man in the regiment, leaving only a few convalescents to guard our camp. The orders for details had all to be copied, the officers in command of squads furnished with instructions, the men thoroughly inspected, and all this labor fell upon the Adjutant, who never seemed to tire. He never allowed a squad of men to leave camp without being thoroughly inspected and every thing in order. No set of officers, with a few exceptions, or men in the service of the United States, ever more faithfully earned their pay than those of the Fourteenth New-Hampshire Regiment.

"The last of June, 1863, the regiment was suddenly called, at half-past eleven o'clock at night, to man the lines at or near Fort Stephens, to repel an expected attack of Stewart's Cavalry, seven thousand strong, who were raiding Maryland north of Washington. At twelve o'clock, midnight, every able-bodied man and officer in camp was in line, and moved at once into the trenches and bivouacked on the lines in front of Fort Stephens. During that night Adjutant Gardiner was by my side, and I had occasion oftentimes to note his coolness and self-collection under the most trying circumstances. Lucky for the enemy, we were not attacked,—although their camp-fires were plainly in view,—as our regiment had become sufficiently disciplined to feel their strength, and were burning to try their hands on the Johnnies.

"Gardiner possessed a winning address, and his pleasant voice and gentlemanly manner won for him favor and respect in high quarters; and when I desired to get some man or men excused at headquarters for some delinquency, I always selected Gardiner to do the business, as he knew well how to time and tone his words for the occasion.

"In September Gardiner was promoted to Major, on my recommendation as the man best fitted for the position, by education, talent, and gentlemanly bearing. After we reached New-Orleans, in April, 1864, Major Gardiner was in command of the regiment much of the time. On the 13th of July we sailed from New-Orleans, leaving Major Gardiner with four companies behind. I only met him again in the Valley of the Shenandoah, at Berryville, on the 19th of August. On the night of August 21st, the army was withdrawn from its position in front of the enemy near Charlestown, Va. The withdrawal of the pickets fell upon Major Gardiner as officer of the day. It was a delicate duty to perform, in the immediate face of the enemy, but was accomplished by him successfully. The lines had not been evacuated more than ten minutes before the enemy charged over our empty breastworks in full force, showing that they were on the alert for our movements. On the 7th of September I received my discharge.

"Major Gardiner was quite a nice man in his dress and personal appearance. He prided himself on wearing the nicest fitting boots in the regiment, and we had many a laugh at the rivalry between Dr. Thayer, Major Gardiner and Adjutant Wright, who all had a weakness toward nice boots. After

Gardiner was wounded and left on the ground at the battle of Opequan Creek, his handsome boots attracted the eye of a Johnnie Reb., who despoiled him of them, causing him great pain and suffering. But Johnnie had but a short lease of the boots, as he was taken prisoner before night and compelled to strip himself of the boots and lug them into camp hung around his neck, himself marching barefooted over the flinty road."

When Col. Wilson was discharged, Brig. Gen. Birge, who was in command of the brigade of which the Fourteenth Regiment formed a part, wrote Gov. Gilmore of this State, requesting Major Gardiner's appointment over the Lieut. Colonel, who had held the office from the formation of the regiment. He wrote—"I am informed that Major Gardiner has been constantly on duty with his regiment since its organization. During the time it has been under my command he has performed the duties of his office with fidelity, ability and zeal, and I believe him well qualified and competent for the rank recommended. In my opinion, his promotion is deserved, and will be for the benefit of the service and the regiment, and creditable to the State which he represents." The recommendation was followed, and Major Gardiner received his commission as Colonel only the day before the battle of Opequan Creek, where he was mortally wounded.

- Col. Gardiner was born in the State of New-York in 1833; graduated at Kimball Union Academy, Meriden, N. H.; studied for the profession of law and was admitted to the bar in New-York city when twenty-two years old; went to Kansas with the intention of establishing himself in his professional business, and to assist in publishing a newspaper. His printing office was destroyed by the border ruffians, and the newspaper was abandoned; he engaged for a time in the border war, and on account of failing health returned home, and came to Claremont in the spring of 1859, and entered into a law partnership with Capt. Edwin Vaughan, of the New-Hampshire Cavalry. * He married a daughter of Hon. Lemuel P. Cooper of Croydon, and sister of Surgeon Sherman Cooper of the 6th Regiment, who, with two children, survive him.

His remains were brought to Claremont and buried with Masonic honors by Hiram Lodge. Prof. E. T. Rowe of Kimball Union Academy, who had been Col. Gardiner's teacher, and was for a time Chaplain of his regiment, preached an appropriate and impressive sermon at the town hall, to a large concourse of people. His horse, with the empty saddle, followed him to the grave.

OLIVER P. GILLINGHAM

Enlisted and was mustered into Co. I, 14th Reg't, Sept. 24, 1862. Discharged for disability at Poolsville, Md., Feb. 5, 1863, and died April 22, 1863.

LEVI D. HALL, Jr.

Enlisted as a recruit, and was mustered into Co. I, 14th Reg't, Jan. 14, 1864. He was a good soldier, and most of the time on duty at Brigade Headquarters. Mustered out at Concord, Aug. 14, 1865.

MARTIN V. B. HURLEY

Enlisted and was mustered into Co. I, 14th Reg't, Sept. 24, 1862. Served faithfully to the end of the war, and was mustered out June 12, 1865.

PATRICK HOBAN

Enlisted and was mustered into Co. I, 14th Reg't, Sept. 24, 1862. Served faithfully, and was mustered out June 8, 1865.

LEVI LEET

Enlisted and was mustered into Co. I, 14th Reg't, as a musician, Sept. 24, 1862. Discharged for disability at Concord, June 26, 1863, and died of disease contracted in the army July 17, 1863.

MITCHELL OLIVER

Enlisted as a recruit, and was mustered into Co. I, 14th Reg't, Dec. 29, 1863. Discharged May 29, 1865, on account of wounds received at Opequan Creek, near Winchester, Va., Sept. 19, 1864. He was shot through both legs, fracturing the bone of the right leg badly. Was a good soldier, faithful in the discharge of every duty.

HENRY S. PAULL

Enlisted and was mustered into Co. I, 14th Reg't, Sept. 24, 1862. Promoted to Sergeant. Promoted to Second Lieutenant Jan. 1, 1864. Promoted to First Lieutenant Feb. 19, 1864. Killed at the battle of Opequan Creek, near Winchester, Va., Sept. 19, 1864. During much of the time that the 14th Reg't was in Washington, Lieut. Paull was on detached duty, and had charge of the Central Guard House in that city several months. Here, as elsewhere, he was a faithful, efficient and most acceptable officer. Soon after the opening of the battle of Opequan Creek, Paull was severely wounded in the leg. A member of his old Co., I, found him helpless upon the field and took him upon his back and was carrying him to the rear when a rebel minnie ball hit Paull in the head, killing him instantly, and he was left sitting by the side of a tree. The enemy took possession of the field, which was soon retaken by our troops, and his body recovered, though it had been stripped of all valuables. He was buried by his men, and his grave marked as best it could be. He was a son of Seth Paull of Claremont, and one of the bravest and best officers of his regiment. A young wife and many friends mourn his early death.

Sergeant GEORGE H. STOWELL

Enlisted and was mustered into Co. I, 14th Reg't, Sept. 24, 1862. Appointed Corporal Jan. 26, 1864. Promoted to Sergeant Jan. 1, 1865. Mustered out with the regiment July 26, 1865. He was detached for recruiting service in this State from July 20, 1863, to Feb. 1864, being senior officer from his regiment, under Lieut. Fosgate. He was in the Opequan Creek battle, and was slightly wounded by a piece of shell. He is a son of Abner Stowell of Claremont. After his muster out he returned home, and is one of the Sugar River Mill Co.

FIFTEENTH REGIMENT.

This was the first regiment raised in New-Hampshire under the call of the President for three hundred thousand nine months men. The field officers were John W. Kingman of Durham, Colonel; George W. Frost of Newmarket, Lieut. Colonel, and Henry W. Blair of Plymouth, Major. The regiment was mustered on the 12th of November, 1862, and ordered to report to Gen. N. P. Banks at New-York. It was in Banks' expedition, and arrived at New-Orleans the last of December. It was engaged in the assault on Port Hudson on the 27th of May, and in the subsequent siege, doing good service and bearing its share of hardships. It returned to Concord and was mustered out on the 13th of August, 1863.

SIXTEENTH REGIMENT.

This was the second nine months regiment organized in New-Hampshire. The field officers were James Pike of Sanbornton, Colonel; Henry W. Fuller of Concord, Lieut. Colonel, and Samuel Davis, Jr., of Warner, Major. The regiment was mustered at Concord the last of Oct. 1862, and ordered to report to Gen. N. P. Banks, at New-York. It joined Gen. Banks' expedition, went to New-Orleans, and thence to Port Hudson. This regiment suffered very much from disease engendered by the climate, and exposure to which the men were unaccustomed. It was engaged in several battles and skirmishes, showing the true New-Hampshire valor. On the 20th of August, having previously returned to Concord, it was mustered out.

SEVENTEENTH REGIMENT.

A portion only of the companies of this regiment were filled. The men were enlisted at the same time as those for the Fifteenth and Sixteenth, for nine months. Henry O. Kent of Lancaster was appointed Colonel; Charles H. Long of Claremont, Lieut. Colonel, and George A. Bellows of Walpole, Major. Soon after the call for nine months regiments, in the summer of 1862, it was determined to raise a regiment in each Congressional District— the Fifteenth in the First, the Sixteenth in the Second, and the Seventeenth in the Third. Before either regiment was filled orders were received to forward the new troops as rapidly as possible, and the Fifteenth and Sixteenth Regiments were filled as fast as men could be enlisted, without regard to the locality from which they came. After the first two regiments had been filled, the rest of the men enlisted were ordered into Camp at Concord on the 19th of November, and put under a regular course of discipline and drill. On the 9th of

February the officers and men were furloughed until the 1st of the succeeding April. When the command reported in camp it was determined to consolidate the Seventeenth with the depleted Second Regiment, which was effected on the 16th of April, 1863. The commissioned and non-commissioned officers of the Seventeenth were mustered out, and the men transferred to the Second. Thus ended this organization.

HARRISON FILLMORE HAWKES

Enlisted and was mustered into Co. I, 17th Reg't, as a musician, Dec. 5, 1862. Transferred to the 2d Reg't, April, 1863. He enlisted for nine months, and was mustered out Oct. 9, 1863. He was in the battle of Gettysburg, and from there went to Point Lookout, to guard rebel prisoners, where he was taken sick with rheumatic fever and chronic diarrhea, and but for the care of his Claremont friends, who were in the same company, must have died. He was very feeble for several months after he came home, but finally recovered, and is now clerk in a leather store in Boston. He is a son of Albert Hawkes of Claremont.

EIGHTEENTH REGIMENT.

Under a call from the War Department for five hundred thousand volunteers, issued July 19, 1864, the recruiting of this regiment was commenced. Joseph M. Clough of New-London was commissioned Lieut. Colonel, and William I. Brown of Fisherville, Major, and in December joined their command, consisting of six companies, which had been sent forward, and were stationed at City Point, Va. These six companies completed the quota of the State, and no others were sent forward until the next call for troops was issued, December 21, 1864. In the months of February, March and April, 1865, the four additional companies were sent forward, and Thomas L. Livermore, Major of the Fifth, was commissioned Colonel. Co. K was never sent to the front, but was stationed at Galloupe's Island, Boston Harbor, where it was mustered out on the 6th of May, 1865. The regiment did good service, and by order of the War Department the names of the following engagements were inscribed upon its colors: Fort Stedman, March 25, 1865. Attack on Petersburg, April 2, 1865. Capture of Petersburg, April 3, 1865. The last company of this regiment was mustered out at Concord on the 8th of August, 1865. No further Infantry regiments were called for by the War Department, and this was the last one raised in this State.

NEW-HAMPSHIRE CAVALRY.

In the autumn of 1861 the Secretary of War authorized the Governors of the six New-England States to raise a cavalry regiment of twelve companies—two from each State—to be called the New-England Cavalry. Subsequently all these States, except Rhode-Island and New-Hampshire, filled each an entire regiment. Rhode-Island raised eight and New-Hampshire four companies, and they were united, making a regiment. David B. Nelson of Manchester was commissioned Major of the New-Hampshire battalion. The captains of the four companies in this State were Steven R. Swett of Andover, Co. I; John L. Thompson of Plymouth, Co. K; John J. Prentiss of Claremont, Co. L; William P. Ainsworth of Nashua, Co. M. On the 22d of December these four companies joined the eight Rhode-Island companies at Pawtucket. On the 14th of March, 1862, the regiment was ordered to Washington and joined the army of the Potomac, and remained with it to the close of the war. While in Washington the name was changed from the First New-England Cavalry to the First Rhode-Island Cavalry. This greatly disaffected the New-Hampshire men, since by this change they had lost their State identity, and were never fully satisfied with it. It proved an unfortunate arrangement for the New-Hampshire battalion, as the Governor, with that state of things, refused to send recruits to fill its ranks, notwithstanding those men in the field had won for themselves an honorable name on more than one occasion. In January, 1864, the New-Hampshire battalion was permanently detached from the First Rhode-Island Cavalry, with a view of forming a New-Hampshire Cavalry regiment. In February the men nearly all reënlisted with this view, and came home on their veteran furlough. Before the close of April the four old companies were filled, and three new ones had been organized. John L. Thompson was commissioned Colonel, B. T. Hutchins, Lieut. Colonel, and Arnold Wyman, J. F. Andrews and J. A. Cummings, Majors. These seven companies were ordered to Washington, and the other five followed as soon as they were filled, and joined the regiment in August. These last five companies were largely composed of men who had come to the State and enlisted for the large bounties then being paid, many of whom deserted on the way to the regiment.

The First Rhode-Island Cavalry was in camp at Warrenton Junction, on the 23d of May, 1862. Gen. Shields, with his army on the march to Fredericksburg, passed that way, and telegraphed to Washington for leave to have this regiment join his command. The War Department answered that he might take from it the best drilled battalion. The officer in command of the regiment, being a Rhode-Island man, said he regretted to feel compelled to award the honor to the New-Hampshire battalion. Thereupon the four companies from this State joined Gen. Shields' army, and marched that night to Fredericksburg, where they remained until the next day, when they marched back past their old camp to Front Royal, about two hundred miles, marching day and night without stopping to camp. Arriving near Front Royal the enemy's camps were in sight, and the indications were that they were about to retreat across the Shenandoah and burn the bridges after them. The battalion was ordered to charge into the town and save the bridges. The battalion consisted at this time of about one hundred and twenty-five effective men. They charged upon, routed and closely pursued for four miles two regiments of rebel infantry, saved the bridges, captured one hundred and fifty-six prisoners, two pieces of artillery, and eleven wagons loaded with quartermaster's stores and camp and garrison equipage. In this charge Capt. Ainsworth and nine men were killed and five wounded. Here the regiment lost its first man in battle. From this time until the close of the war our cavalry were engaged in the well remembered Wilson and Stoneman raids, Sheridan's celebrated campaign in the Shenandoah Valley, in the fall of 1864, and indeed was always in the field and identified with all the movements and battles in which the cavalry of the army of the Potomac was engaged.

In February, 1865, the seven companies of this regiment, together with some men from other cavalry regiments, making a force in all of about six hundred men, under Col. Thompson, was detailed to take twelve hundred prisoners of Early's army from Waynesborough to Winchester, one hundred and twenty-five miles, which he accomplished, adding over a hundred to his number of prisoners on the march. He was harrassed all the way by a rebel brigade of cavalry. Gen. Emery did Col. Thompson the honor to say that "the taking of Early's army at Waynesborough was a big thing; but the bringing of the prisoners back to Winchester, by Col. Thompson, was a great deal bigger thing." Gen. Sheridan, afterward, when asked if he expected those prisoners to be taken safely to Winchester, said, "No; but I knew Thompson would take them there if any body could."

It would be interesting to follow this regiment in the many ventures, charges and battles in which it distinguished itself, if the limits of this book would permit it. Suffice to say that the New-Hampshire battalion, and subsequently the New-Hampshire regiment of cavalry, bore a conspicuous part in cavalry movements in the army of the Potomac with distinguished bravery, coolness and honor. The regiment returned to New-Hampshire and was mustered out July 21, 1865.

Corporal HENRY G. AYER

Enlisted at Manchester and was mustered into Troop K, New-England Cavalry, Oct. 24, 1861. Promoted to Corporal. Served to the end of his term of enlistment and was mustered out Oct. 24, 1864. In the fall of 1862 he was detailed as Clerk for the Quartermaster of the regiment, and when that officer was promoted to Brigade Quartermaster, Corp. Ayer was taken with him as Clerk. He was subsequently detailed as Clerk in the Cavalry

Bureau at Washington, where he remained until his term of enlistment expired. He is a son of Rev. Oliver Ayer, lately of Claremont, but now settled at Groton, Mass., and was an efficient and faithful soldier.

CHARLES S. ALLEN

Enlisted and was mustered into Troop L, New-England Cavalry, Dec. 27, 1861, and appointed Wagoner. Reënlisted for a second term of three years, Jan. 5, 1864. He was a most efficient and faithful wagoner, always cool and collected under whatever circumstances of difficulty or danger. It has been said of him by those in his company, that from a very small beginning he would very soon get together a good six mule team. He was mustered out with his regiment, and now runs a team from Claremont to the railroad depot.

ETHAN A. BALLOU

Enlisted and was mustered into Troop I, First New-England Cavalry, Dec. 17, 1861. Discharged for disability April 19, 1862. Enlisted and was mustered into the Veteran Reserve Corps, Jan. 31, 1865, where he served until the end of the war, and was mustered out Nov. 7, 1865.

Sergeant WILLIAM H. BRIGGS

Enlisted and was mustered into Troop L, New-England Cavalry, Dec. 27, 1861. Promoted to Sergeant. Wounded in the side by a piece of shell at the battle of Chantilly, Sept. 1, 1862. He was subsequently injured in another action, and was discharged on account of injuries received in battle, Jan. 16, 1862. After his discharge he was appointed Superintendent of the Government Wood-yard at Washington, which position he retained about two years, when he returned home, and is now engaged in the manufacture of cabinet furniture.

FRANCIS CLARK

Enlisted and was mustered into Troop L, New-England Cavalry, Jan. 8, 1862. Transferred to Veteran Reserve Corps, Nov. 15, 1863.

WILLIAM H. FARWELL

Enlisted and was mustered into Troop L, New-England Cavalry, Dec. 27, 1861. Discharged for disability, Dec. 5, 1862.

LEWIS W. LADUCER

Enlisted under Capt. Austin for three months, in April, 1861, went to Portsmouth, but did not reënlist for three years, and was discharged. Enlisted and was mustered into Troop L, New-England Cavalry, Dec. 27, 1861. Was also in Troop L, New-Hampshire Cavalry. Sent to Lincoln General Hospital, Washington, D. C., which is the last report of him. His term of enlistment expired Dec. 27, 1864.

WILLIAM H. H. MOODY

Enlisted and was mustered into Troop L, New-England Cavalry, Dec. 27, 1861. Discharged by order, Jan. 18, 1862.

Sergeant EDWARD F. MOORE

Enlisted and was mustered into Co. L, First New-England Cavalry, Dec. 27, 1861. He was soon appointed Corporal. Once when sent out with a party of skirmishers they were surprised by Stewart's rebel cavalry, and after great efforts to escape was taken prisoner. Soon after being exchanged he was appointed Chief Orderly in Gen. Humphrey's escort. He was in the thickest of the fight at Fredericksburg, Dec. 13, 1862, and saw one hundred and fifty of his comrades fall in five minutes. He was in all the battles with his company, without injury to himself or horse, until the terrible battle of Gettysburg, July 2, 1863, when he was struck by a piece of shell and instantly killed. His funeral was largely attended at the Methodist church, on Sunday, Aug. 9th, Rev. Mr. Hartwell officiating. He was a son of Edward W. Moore of Claremont; was born in Andover, Mass., in 1841, where his father then lived, but came to this town about fourteen years ago. He was an intelligent and excellent young man, and a brave and noble soldier.

Sergeant ELI C. MARSH

Enlisted and was mustered into Troop L, New-England Cavalry, Dec. 27, 1861. Appointed Regimental Commissary Sergeant. Transferred to Veteran Reserve Corps, March 1, 1863.

HENRY H. NILES

Enlisted and was mustered into Troop L, New-England Cavalry, Dec. 27, 1861. Discharged for disability, June 16, 1862. Enlisted into Veteran Reserve Corps, Aug. 25, 1864. Mustered out Nov. 7, 1865.

Captain JOHN J. PRENTISS

Was commissioned Captain of Co. L, New-England Cavalry, Dec. 3, 1861. After being in the field a few months, and soon after the battle at Culpeper Court House, he was detailed on recruiting service, to fill the Rhode-Island Cavalry, which name the regiment, to which the four companies from this State was attached, had taken after reaching the field. Without returning to his regiment he was discharged Nov. 3, 1863. He is the father of Capt. William P. Prentiss of Troop K, New-Hampshire Cavalry, and John J. Prentiss, Jr., of the 5th Regiment, of whom honorable mention is made elsewhere.

Captain WILLIAM PARKER PRENTISS

Was commissioned Second Lieutenant of Co. L, New-Hampshire Battalion First New-England Cavalry, Dec. 3, 1861. Promoted to First Lieutenant, Aug. 4, 1862. Promoted to Captain, April 21, 1864, and assigned to Co. K, First New-Hampshire Cavalry. Resigned and was mustered out Jan. 18, 1865. He was almost constantly with his company, and participated in all its battles, raids and skirmishes, until the regiment came home on its veteran furlough, in February, 1864. Soon after its arrival at Concord Lieut. Prentiss was ordered to Claremont on recruiting service, where he remained until the 21st of April, when he was promoted to Captain, rejoined his regiment, and on the 25th started with it for the front. In November, 1864, he was appointed acting Adjutant and Inspector General to Col. Provost, at the Draft

Rendezvous, Springfield, Ill., and on the 28th of the following December was assigned to duty on General Court Marshal at Winchester, Va., in which position he remained until his resignation was accepted. He was with the regiment on the celebrated Wilson Raid, which was unequaled during the war, either in hardships or results, and here, as on all other occasions, exhibited great coolness and bravery. It is only necessary to refer to the history of his regiment to know what part he took in the war of the rebellion. He was almost always with his command, and bore his full share in their hard marches, bloody battles, and almost unprecedented privations and hardships. He several times lost his horse, sabre, all his equipments and cap; went through the fight at Middleburg bareheaded; was repeatedly reported killed, wounded, and prisoner; got many bullet-holes through his garments, but was never seriously wounded. While he was generally where the battle raged fiercest he seemed to bear a charmed life, and when his men and fellow-officers were shot down all around him, he was protected by a kind Providence from harm at the hands of the rebels. Capt. Prentiss was an officer of more than ordinary ability, devoted to his duty in whatever position placed, and commanded the respect and confidence of all the men and officers with whom he was connected. It was such men as he who gained for our New-Hampshire Cavalry the enviable reputation it always enjoyed. He is a brother of John J. Prentiss, Jr., of the 5th Regiment, and is now living in Chicago. Both are sons of Capt. John J. Prentiss, of the New-England Cavalry.

CHARLES E. PATRICK,

First New-England Cavalry, son of William Patrick. Mustered into Troop L, Dec. 27, 1861. Promoted to Sergeant. Reënlisted Jan. 5, 1864. Promoted to First Lieutenant April 15, 1864. Promoted to Captain June 19, 1865, but was never mustered on this commission. Mustered out as First Lieutenant July 15, 1865, and returned home. He subsequently went to South-Carolina and entered into business there.

Sergeant OTIS G. ROBINSON

Enlisted and was mustered into Troop L, New-England Cavalry, Dec. 27, 1861. Promoted to Sergeant. Discharged for disability Sept. 14, 1862.

SAMUEL J. SAWYER

Enlisted and was mustered into Co. K, Rhode-Island Cavalry, Oct. 4, 1862. Served to the end of the war and was mustered out with the regiment.

Corporal GEORGE W. SLEEPER

Enlisted and was mustered into Troop L, New-England Cavalry. Appointed Corporal. Wounded severely March 17, 1863. Mustered out Dec. 27, 1864. He was a brave soldier.

BENJAMIN W. STILL

Enlisted and was mustered into Troop L, New-England Cavalry, Dec. 27, 1861. Was severely injured while in Rhode-Island, by his horse falling upon him, and was discharged in consequence, June 4, 1862.

Corporal JAMES M. SOUTHWICK

Enlisted and was mustered into Troop L, New-England Cavalry, Dec. 27, 1861. Promoted to Corporal. Reënlisted Jan. 5, 1864. Most of the time he acted as Wagoner, and is said to have been one of the best men in his regiment. At the close of the war he was mustered out, came home, and now resides in Claremont.

Captain EDWIN VAUGHAN

Enlisted and was mustered into Troop L, First New-England Cavalry, Dec. 13, 1861. Appointed Sergeant before the First New-Hampshire battalion left the State. Promoted to Second Lieutenant Aug. 15, 1862, and assigned to Co. C. Promoted to First Lieutenant Jan. 1, 1863, and assigned to Co. G, and a portion of the time was Adjutant of the regiment. Promoted to Captain March 31, 1864, and assigned to the command of Co. A. The latter part of 1863 and the first part of 1864, he was detailed on the Staff of the Brigade Commander as acting Assistant Adjutant General. He was continually with his regiment from the time of his enlistment until the 12th of August, 1864. When on Wilson's Raid, in June, 1864, Capt. Vaughan was partially sun-struck, but remained with his regiment until the following August, when he was obliged to go into hospital, and remained in hospitals at Georgetown and Annapolis until November, when he was detailed as Assistant Provost Marshal of the 8th Army Corps and assigned to duty at Baltimore, where he remained until the 7th of June, 1865, when, by special order of the War Department, he was discharged. While in the field he was continually with his command, and it is only necessary to refer to its history for an account of the marches, sieges, raids and battles in which he participated. In January, 1864, Capt. Vaughan reënlisted three quarters of the men in his regiment. In the fall of 1861 he was appointed Captain in the 7th Regiment, but on account of sickness in his family was obliged to decline it. While Assistant Provost Marshal he won for himself the respect and confidence of all with whom he was connected. John Woolley, Provost Marshal General of the Middle Military Department, wrote of him: "Capt. Vaughan reported to me and was assigned to duty as Assistant Provost Marshal in charge of the Pass Office and Prison Department. Very frequently he was called upon to make important arrests, examine cases of spies, blockade runners, deserters and bounty jumpers, in all of which he was called upon to display not a little skill and judgment. The conviction, sentence and imprisonment of many of the worst enemies of the country is due to the efforts of Capt. Vaughan. His prompt attention to the demands of those with whom he came in contact, and the full, ample justice rendered by him to all, secured to him the reputation of being one of the best executive officers in the Department."

Brevet Brig. Gen. Horace Benney Sargent, formerly Colonel of the First Massachusetts Cavalry, wrote to Capt. Vaughan, under date of March 17, 1868: "In connection with an intimation that New-Hampshire is to have a war record from Claremont, I should be glad to recognize my debt to a splendid regiment in which you served, and to you as a most efficient Staff Officer of my Cavalry Brigade, when we both served Gen. Duffié. And as a part of the process you will allow me to express to you my full sense of your merits as a brave, faithful, reliable and constant Aid, whose hand and heart I never had an instant's cause to doubt, and gratefully recollect."

FIRST LIGHT BATTERY.

This battery was recruited and organized at Manchester, and mustered on the 26th of September, 1861. It numbered one hundred and fifty men, and was completely armed and equipped as a six gun battery. The officers were George A. Gerrish of Portsmouth, Captain; Fred. M. Edgell of Orford, First Lieutenant, and John Wadleigh and Henry F. Condit of Manchester, Second Lieutenants. It was assigned to the army of the Potomac, with which it remained during the war, being engaged in many battles and doing noble service in all of them. In October, 1864, it was attached to the New-Hampshire Heavy Artillery, but detailed to serve as light artillery, and continued in the field. In speaking of this battery the Adjutant General's Report for 1866 says — "It was not excelled for intelligence, courge or endurance by any company in service, and uniformly received the compliments of the officers under whom it chanced to serve."

It returned to New-Hampshire and was mustered out in June, 1865. There were no Claremont men in this organization.

HEAVY ARTILLERY.

The first two companies of this regiment were raised in the summer of 1863, under special authority of the War Department, to garrison the defenses of Portsmouth harbor. Charles H. Long of Claremont was commissioned Captain of Co. A, and Ira McL. Barton Captain of Co. B. Capt. Long's company was stationed at Fort Constitution, and Capt. Barton's at Fort McClary, Kittery Point, where they remained until May, 1864, when they were assigned to duty in the defenses of Washington. In August authority was granted New-Hampshire to raise a battalion, and subsequently a regiment of Heavy Artillery. After eleven companies had been sent forward, the Light Battery was attached, which filled the regiment, and Capt. Long was commissioned Colonel, Capt. Barton Lieut. Colonel, and George A. Wainwright of Hanover, and Dexter G. Reed of Newport, Majors. The regiment remained in the defenses of Washington, garrisoning a line of works ten miles in extent, until the close of the war. The history of this organization is a. somewhat uneventful one, though it performed important and at times arduous duties. It returned to New-Hampshire and was mustered out on the 19th of June, 1865.

OSCAR BOOTH

Enlisted and was mustered into Co. A, Heavy Artillery, Nov. 26, 1864. Mustered out with the regiment, Sept. 11, 1865.

ALVARO L. CHAFFIN

Enlisted and was mustered into Co. A, Heavy Artillery, Aug. 5, 1864. Served to the end of the war, and was mustered out with the regiment.

GILBERT F. COLBY

Enlisted and was mustered into Co. A, Heavy Artillery, Sept. 24, 1864. Served to the end of the war, and was mustered out Sept. 11, 1865.

GEORGE E. FORD

Enlisted at Fairfield, Me., Aug. 8, 1861, for three years, was mustered into Co. E, 7th Maine Regiment and appointed Sergeant. He was in all the battles of the Peninsular Campaign against Richmond, under Gen. McClellan, until after the Seven Days' Battle, when he was detailed to assist in removing the sick and wounded to Washington and Georgetown, and served as nurse in one of the hospitals until October, 1862, when he was discharged for disability. He enlisted again and was mustered into Co. A, New-Hampshire Heavy Artillery, May 26, 1863. Deserted at Fort Constitution, March 27, 1864. He afterward enlisted and served in Battery F, First Missouri Artillery to the end of the war. Son of the late Rev. J. W. Ford, and brother of James B. Ford, who served in the 1st and 7th Maine Regiments, and Lieut. Charles P. Ford of the 76th New-York Regiment.

WARREN H. GOULD

Enlisted and was mustered into Co. B, Heavy Artillery, Sept. 7, 1863. Mustered out with regiment, Sept. 11, 1865.

Colonel CHARLES H. LONG

Was commissioned Captain of Co. G, 5th Reg't, Oct. 12, 1861; wounded severely in the arm at the battle of Antietam, Sept. 17, 1862, and resigned to receive promotion, Nov. 6, 1862. On the breaking out of the war, Col. Long, having graduated at

Norwich, Vt., Military University, in 1855, offered his services to the State to drill recruits, was thus engaged at Newport, Concord, Dover, Portsmouth, and other places, until July, 1861, when he opened an office in Claremont, and commenced recruiting a company for the 5th Regiment. He soon obtained the requisite number of men and took them into camp at Concord. On resigning his commission as Captain in the 5th Regiment, he was commissioned Lieut. Colonel of the 17th, a nine months regiment, then being recruited in the 3d Congressional District. A portion of the men enlisted for this were taken to fill the 15th and 16th Regiments, the residue were put into the 2d, and this organization was abandoned in April, 1863. April 17, 1863, he was commissioned Captain, and authorized to raise a company of Heavy Artillery to garrison the defenses of Portsmouth. This company was mustered into the United States service in June and July. After a few months' service at Fort Constitution, this and another company, which had been raised for the same purpose, was ordered to the defenses of Washington. A full regiment of Heavy Artillery was raised in this State, in the summer of 1864, and Long was commissioned Colonel Sept. 29, 1864. He remained in the defenses of Washington with his command until after the close of the war, and was mustered out with his regiment, in June, 1865. In November Col. Long was ordered to the command of the First Brigade, Hardin's Division, 22d Army Corps, and continued in this position until mustered out. In regard to his record as an officer, Gen. Caldwell wrote—"Col. Charles H. Long, 1st New-Hampshire Heavy Artillery, served as Captain in the 5th New-Hampshire Volunteers, of my brigade, from Fair Oaks until after the battle of Antietam. I knew him well, and always esteemed him one of the best Captains I knew. He was prompt, gallant and efficient, and an ornament to the service. Perfectly reliable as a man and an officer, I frequently selected him for enterprises requiring judgment and ability, and he always discharged his duties to my entire satisfaction." Major General Howard, Brig. General Hardin, and other officers under whom he served, speak of him and his military services in commendatory terms. At the end of the war Capt. Long returned to Claremont, and is now living upon the farm where he was born.

ALBERT NEWCOMB

Enlisted and was mustered into Co. A, Heavy Artillery, Aug. 3, 1864. Mustered out with the regiment, Sept. 11, 1865.

WILLIAM L. PARKHURST

Enlisted and was mustered into Co. A, Heavy Artillery, July 2, 1863. Mustered out with the regiment, Sept. 11, 1865.

Corporal FRANCIS RAFFERTY

Enlisted and was mustered into Co. A, Heavy Artillery, Dec. 26, 1863. Promoted to Corporal Nov. 1, 1864. Mustered out Sept. 11, 1865.

DANIEL B. SMITH

Enlisted and was mustered into Co. A, Heavy Artillery, May 26, 1863. Mustered out Sept. 14, 1865.

HARVEY D. STONE

Enlisted and was mustered into Co. A, Heavy Artillery, Sept. 15, 1863. Mustered out of the service with his regiment, Sept. 11, 1865.

GEORGE H. WALDRON

Enlisted and was mustered into Co. B, Heavy Artillery, Sept. 15, 1863. Mustered out with regiment, Sept. 11, 1865.

SHARP-SHOOTERS.

New-Hampshire furnished three full companies for this arm of the service. Two regiments, known as Berdan's Sharp-shooters, were raised by authority of the War Department, of which the companies from this State formed a part. The men for these companies, and especially the first one, which was afterward designated as Co. E, were selected with reference to their skill as marksmen with the rifle at long range, and embraced some of the best rifle-shots in the State, and all were good men. The test for admission into this organization, established by the War Department, was that "each man was to make a string of ten shots, measuring in the aggregate, from center of bull's-eye to center of ball, not more than fifty inches, at a distance of one hundred yards, off-hand, or two hundred yards at a rest." The strings of the first company varied from seven to thirty inches. The officers of this company were Amos B. Jones of Washington, Captain; William P. Austin of Claremont, First Lieut., and William H. Gibbs of Hanover, Second Lieutenant. It was mustered on the 9th of September, 1861, and soon after went into a camp of instruction near Washington. Soon after two other companies were raised and sent forward, and Capt. Jones was commissioned Major, and Lieut. Austin was promoted to Captain of Co. E. The battalion was attached to the Second Regiment of United States Sharp-shooters. This was found to be a very efficient organization. The Adjutant General's Report for 1866 says of them: "They participated in more battles and skirmishes than the average of regiments, and probably killed more rebels than the same number of troops in any other arm of the service; while from their being seldom used in line of battle, in dense masses, they suffered less loss in comparison than many other regiments." Early in April they went to Yorktown, where they distinguished themselves in the first battle of the campaign, crawling up near the rebel works and picking off the rebel gunners so surely as to render their batteries nearly useless. It was in this engagement that Co. E lost its first man, killed, John S. M. Ide of Claremont. During the entire siege of Yorktown the Sharpshooters rendered great service. They were also engaged at the second Bull Run, where Capt. W.

P. Austin was badly wounded in the arm. The Sharp-shooters remained with the army of the Potomac during the war, and participated in most of its battles. Co. E was allowed, by different commanding Generals under which it served, to inscribe upon its colors the names and dates of thirty different actions in which it was engaged. On the 8th of September, those men of this company who had not reënlisted were mustered out. Subsequently the men of the battalion who had reënlisted were put into infantry regiments and served to the end of the war.

Captain WILLIAM P. AUSTIN

Was the first man in Claremont to offer his services to the Government in the war of the rebellion. On the 18th of April, 1861, he enlisted as a private, under the call of President Lincoln for seventy-five thousand volunteers for three months. On the same day he was appointed recruiting officer for Claremont and vicinity, and immediately opened an office here. In a few days he had enlisted eighty-five good and true young men, the most of whom belonged in Claremont. By authority from the Adjutant General the men were allowed to elect their own officers, and William P. Austin was chosen Captain, unanimously. On the

30th of the same month he took his eighty-five men to Concord, and it was conceded by all that it was the finest company that had made its appearance there. They were from the farms, work-shops and stores of Claremont, and had been accepted by Capt. Austin on account of their soldierly qualities. The company reflected great credit upon the town and upon the officer who had recruited it. On the arrival of this company at Concord it was found that more than men enough for one regiment had already gone into camp there, and it had been determined that the Second Regiment should be organized at Portsmouth, and the Claremont company was sent there. Before the Second Regiment was organized an order came from the War Department to send from New-Hampshire one regiment of three months men, and enlist another regiment for three years, to be held subject to orders from Washington. A part only of the Claremont company reënlisted for three years, while a part of the residue were discharged by the examining surgeon, and the balance were sent to Fort Constitution to do garrison duty until the expiration of their term of enlistment. This of course broke up the Claremont company, and none of the officers chosen were commissioned. Capt. Austin was discharged, but went to Washington with the

Second Regiment, where he remained a few days and then returned home. In August Capt. Austin was commissioned First Lieutenant of the first company of Sharp-shooters from New-Hampshire, which was afterward attached to Berdan's Regiment of Sharp-shooters, and was lettered E. While at Camp of Instruction, Dec. 20, 1861, he was promoted to Captain of the same company. He was with his company in every action until that of the second Bull Run, on the 30th of August, 1862, where he received a severe wound from a rifle ball in the right arm, just below the elbow. He was carried to Washington, where he remained in hospital twelve weeks, when he came home on furlough. He reported to the War Department, Washington, in May, 1863, resigned on account of his wound, and was honorably discharged on the 16th of that month. On the 13th of August, 1863, he was appointed Captain of the Invalid Corps, which soon took the name of the Veteran Reserve Corps, and assigned to duty at Rutland, Vt., and was afterward called to Portsmouth Grove Hospital, Rhode-Island, where he was Military Assistant one year. The first of October, 1864, he joined his regiment at Galloupe's Island, Boston Harbor, which was the general rendezvous of recruits and substitutes from Maine, New-Hampshire and Massachusetts. The duty there was to bring recruits and substitutes to the Island, guard and conduct them to the front, which, in view of their desperate character and the prejudice existing against the Veteran Reserve Corps, was often trying and hazardous. In March, 1865, he was appointed acting Assistant Quartermaster and Ordnance officer of the Post, and in July Post Commissary, and held these offices until the Island was given up by the Government, in March, 1866. He was member of a General Court Martial convened in Boston from February to May, when he was ordered to report to the Commissioner of the Bureau of Refugees, Freedmen and Abandoned Lands, and assigned to duty in Virginia. In July he was appointed Superintendent of the First District of Virginia, comprising eighteen counties in the south-western part of the State, and stationed at Wytheville, where he was in the summer of 1868. Capt. Austin has rendered varied and important service to the country from April, 1861, to the present time. He is a gentleman of intelligence and worth, honored alike in civil and military life.

EDWARD E. FRENCH

Enlisted and was mustered into Co. E, Berdan's Sharp-shooters, Sept. 9, 1861. He was mortally wounded at the battle of Cold Harbor, Va., June 19, 1864, and died of his wounds Sept. 7, 1864. He came to Claremont about a year before the breaking out of the rebellion, from St. Johnsbury, Vt., where his relatives now reside. He left a young wife.

TIMOTHY GRANNIS

Enlisted and was mustered into Co. E, Berdan's Sharp-shooters, Sept. 9, 1861. He died suddenly in camp at Washington, D. C., Jan. 31, 1862. A comrade wrote to his brother—"He died very suddenly in his tent this morning, Jan. 31. He had been unwell for a day or two, but was out as usual. He got up this morning, made a fire, and was sitting by it, when he was observed to lie down suddenly. He was spoken to, but made no reply, and soon expired. He was a fine young man and very much respected in camp." He was a native of Claremont, son of Laurence A. Grannis, who a few years since removed to the northern part of Vermont. His remains were brought to Claremont and buried in the family lot at the west part of the town.

JOHN S. M. IDE

Enlisted and was mustered into Co. E, Berdan's Sharp-shooters, Sept. 9, 1861. Killed in the engagement before Yorktown, April 5, 1862. He, with others of his company, was placed in a position to pick off the rebel gunners, and did good service. He was shot in the head and instantly expired. When he fell Lieut. Colonel Ripley, of the Vermont Sharp-shooters, took Ide's rifle, and saying he "had a license to shoot that man," fired, and the rebel that killed Mr. Ide bit the dust. A correspondent in describing the scene says—" Thus fell Mr. Ide, with his armor on, in the thickest of the fight. He could not have died a nobler death, and his comrades will always remember how his example stimulated them, and while they have a country to be saved, will pray that if they are to die, their last end may be like his." Capt. William P. Austin, in a letter to his friends in Claremont, wrote—"Mr. Ide's body was put into a house which stood in range of the enemy's guns, and the shells came so thick and fast that the men who were detailed to care for the wounded left the house and did not dare return to it. When I was relieved I took four men and carried his body to where the regiment was in camp, which was about one mile in the rear. The next morning we buried his remains in good order." Mr. Ide was the first man killed among the Sharp-shooters. He was born in Windsor, Vt., in 1829. His father died when John was but an infant, and when ten years old his mother also died, leaving him an orphan, without brother or sister. During his minority he came to Claremont to reside with his relatives, and this town was ever after his home. He was a printer by profession, and was several years in the employ of the Claremont Manufacturing Co. He married a daughter of Simeon Ide, who died four or five years before the breaking out of the rebellion, leaving one son, who was about eight years old at the time of his father's death.

CHARLES M. JUDD

Enlisted under Capt. Austin, in April, 1861, for three months, and was discharged at Portsmouth on account of the loss of an eye. He again enlisted and was mustered into Co. E, Berdan's Sharp-shooters, Sept. 9, 1861. Discharged for disability, Nov. 1, 1862. He again enlisted into the Veteran Reserve Corps, Sept. 9, 1864, and was mustered out Nov. 7, 1865. He was a true and faithful soldier.

WILLIAM H. NICHOLS

Enlisted under Capt. Austin, for three months, in April, 1861. Reënlisted at Portsmouth for three years, detailed for cook, was not mustered, and was discharged when the regiment left the State for Washington. He again enlisted and was mustered into Co. E, Berdan's Sharp-shooters, Sept. 9, 1861. After the second Bull Run battle, went to Washington with wounded men and was detailed for duty at Mount Pleasant Hospital, Washington, appointed Ward Master, and remained there nine months, when he returned to the regiment and participated in all the battles where his company was engaged until his term of enlistment expired, when he came to Concord, with sixteen others, and was mustered out Sept. 8, 1864. He was an excellent and faithful nurse, a good soldier, and is a worthy man.

RUEL G. OSGOOD

Enlisted and was mustered into Co. G, Berdan's Sharp-shooters, Dec. 12, 1861. Discharged for disability April 27, 1862.

HENRY S. PARMALEE

Enlisted and was mustered into Co. E, Berdan's Sharp-shooters, Sept. 9, 1861. Discharged for disability at Washington, Jan. 21, 1862.

HENRY A. REDFIELD

Enlisted and was mustered into Co. G, Berdan's Sharp-shooters, Dec. 12, 1861. Discharged at Washington for disability, Dec. 22, 1862.

CHESTER P. SMITH

Enlisted and was mustered into Co. G, Berdan's Sharp-shooters, Dec. 12, 1861. Discharged for disability May 12, 1862.

GEORGE W. STRAW

Enlisted under Capt. Austin for three months, and declining to enlist for three years was discharged and came home. Enlisted again and was mustered into Co. E, Berdan's Sharp-shooters, Sept. 9, 1861. Appointed Wagoner Oct. 1, 1861. Taken prisoner at Spottsylvania Court House, May 8, 1864, and taken to Richmond. On the 8th of June was taken from Richmond to Andersonville prison, and from there to Mellen, S. C., where he was paroled in December, 1864, and sent to Annapolis. Came home on a furlough, and was discharged at Concord, Jan. 25, 1865.

HORACE W. WHITNEY

Enlisted and was mustered into Co. E, Berdan's Sharp-shooters, Sept. 9, 1861. Promoted to Corporal, Dec. 3, 1861. Discharged at Washington, for disability, March 14, 1862.

NINTH REGIMENT VERMONT INFANTRY.

Since six of Claremont's best men were connected with this regiment, it seems important to their record that its operations should be noted in this history. The regiment was organized and went to the seat of war in July 1862. Charles Jarvis, only son of the late William Jarvis of Weathersfield—almost as well known in Claremont as in his own school district, and enjoying the highest respect of all—had determined from purely patriotic motives and a high sense of duty, to enter the army, and offered his services to the State. He was tendered the command of a regiment, which he declined, as he did also other positions which might seem to some more honorable, to accept authority to raise a company of men in his own town and neighborhood, for the Ninth Regiment of Volunteer Infantry, to be commanded by himself. Good men flocked to his standard, among the best of whom were six from Claremont: Algernon Marble Squier, Albert F. Russell, George W. Davis, Leonard M. Stevens, George W. Spaulding, and Albert E. Parmalee. And it is a curious and most gratifying fact connected with these men and this regiment, that while scarcely a hundred of the original members returned and were mustered out with it, five of the six from Claremont served the full time, came home without a scratch, and were honorably discharged with the regiment in June, 1865. Parmalee was discharged for disability early in 1863, but soon recovered. Squier died in July, 1867—the other five are alive and well.

This regiment was a part of the eleven thousand and five hundred troops disgracefully, and it was feared treacherously, surrendered by Col. Miles, an experienced regular army officer, to Stonewall Jackson, at Harper's Ferry, on the 15th of September, 1862. They were paroled and sent to Chicago, but not exchanged until December. The Ninth Vermont remained at Chicago until April, 1863, when it was sent to City Point with three thousand rebel prisoners. Subsequently it was engaged in the siege of Suffolk and the Peninsular campaign in the summer of 1863. In the fall the regiment went to Newport, N. C., where it remained through the winter. Capt. Jarvis had been promoted to

Major. On the 1st of December he went on a scout with a party of cavalry, and was killed near Cedar Point, N. C. The regiment remained in Newport and vicinity until the fall of 1864, when it went to Bermuda Hundred, attached to the 18th Army Corps, engaged in all the battles on the approach to Richmond, and was among the first to enter that city on the 3d of April, 1865. It remained there until June, when it was sent home to be mustered out.

GEORGE W. DAVIS

Enlisted into Co. D, Capt. Charles Jarvis, 9th Vermont, in June, 1862. Was detailed for duty at the regimental hospital, which he performed most acceptably much of the time he was in the army, and was mustered out with the regiment in June, 1865. He is now in Vermont at work at his trade as a blacksmith.

ALBERT E. PARMALEE

Enlisted under Capt. Austin for three months, in April, 1861, and served out his term of enlistment at Fort Constitution. Enlisted and was mustered into Co. D, Capt. Charles Jarvis, 9th Regiment Vermont Volunteer Infantry, in June, 1862.

Taken prisoner at Winchester, Va., Sept. 2, 1862, while sick in hospital, was carried to Woodstock, Va., where he remained two or three weeks, when he was paroled and sent to Columbus, Ohio. Soon after he was exchanged, discharged for disability and came home.

Sergeant ALBERT F. RUSSELL

Enlisted under Capt. Austin for three months, in April, 1861; went to Portsmouth, and declining to enlist for three years was sent to Fort Constitution to serve out the term of his enlistment. In June, 1862, he enlisted in Capt. Charles Jarvis' Co. D, 9th Vermont Reg't, for three years, and was made Sergeant when the company was organized. He followed the fortunes of the regiment, participating in its hard marches and bloody battles, nobly and patriotically performing every duty, and was mustered out with the regiment in June, 1865. When the army entered Richmond, on the 3d of April, 1865, Russell was in the advance picket line, and he and Geo. W. Spaulding from Claremont were the first two to enter the city. His account of what occurred there at that time is most thrilling and interesting. He is a son of Alonzo R. Russell of Claremont, and now resides here.

GEORGE W. SPAULDING

Enlisted under Capt. Charles Jarvis into Co. D, 9th Vermont Volunteer Infantry, in June, 1862. Taken prisoner with Albert E. Parmalee, and was paroled and returned to the regiment with him, in December, 1862, and was exchanged in January, 1863. He served the full term of his enlistment, and was mustered out June 13, 1865. He was a good soldier from first to last. He was detailed for hospital duty, which he performed acceptably for near two years.

LEONARD M. STEVENS

Enlisted and was mustered into Co. D, Capt. Charles Jarvis, 9th Vermont Volunteer Infantry, June, 1862. He served faithfully until after the close of the war, was mustered out with his regiment, returned to his home in Claremont, and afterward removed with his family to Unity. While at Chicago he was two months in the small-pox hospital, but escaped without taking the disease. In June, 1863, he was detailed for duty in the regimental hospital, and remained there fourteen months. Those men who went from Claremont in the same regiment with him agree that he was a brave and faithful soldier, performing every duty cheerfully, and tenderly, affectionately and faithfully caring for his sick and wounded companions.

ALGERNON MARBLE SQUIER

Enlisted and was mustered as a private into Co. D, Capt. Charles Jarvis, 9th Vermont Volunteer Infantry, in June, 1862, for three years, or during the war. He was soon appointed Hospital Steward, which place he filled most acceptably until January, 1865, when he was discharged for the purpose of enlisting into the Regular Army and occupying the same office. At the end of the war he was assigned a position in the Army Medical Museum at Washington. While there, beside performing the duties required of him, he pursued the study of medicine, and graduated at the Georgetown Medical College, March 5, 1867. He then received the appointment of Assistant Surgeon in the U. S. Army, and was sent to Fort Leavenworth, Kansas. When the cholera broke out at Fort Harker, he was sent there, thence to Fort Larned, where he died of that dreadful disease, on the 29th of July, 1867, after an illness of ten hours. A letter from the commandant at Fort Larned to his mother, informing her of the particulars of the death of her son, says—"The Doctor came to the Post in company with the 18th Kansas Volunteers, and labored assiduously in battling that terrible disease, the cholera, and by his exertions and skill saved the lives of a number of men sick with it; but on the 29th of July he was suddenly taken ill, and in spite of all the exertions of the Post Surgeon, Dr. Marston, who attended him constantly, died in about five hours." While at Washington in the Army Medical Museum, Dr. Squier was detailed by special request of Dr. Woodhull, who had the matter in charge, to assist in compiling a "Catalogue of the Surgical Section of the Army Medical Museum," a work of great value to the surgical profession, and his principal speaks in the highest terms of the value of his services in that work. On hearing of Dr. Squier's death, the Class of 1867, Medical Department Georgetown College, and the clerks of the Surgeon General's office, Washington, D. C., held meetings and adopted resolutions highly complimentary to him, and of sympathy with his afflicted parents and friends. Dr. Squier was born in Felicity, Clermont County, Ohio, Oct. 25, 1842, and removed to Claremont in 1861, with his parents. His father is Dr. W. C. Squier. He was a young man of unusual excellence and promise.

OTHER VERMONT REGIMENTS.

ASHER S. BURBANK

Enlisted and was mustered into Co. A, 4th Vermont Infantry, July 8, 1863. Was in the battle of the Wilderness from the 2d to the 9th of May, 1864, Spottsylvania, Cold Harbor, Siege of Petersburg, and was taken prisoner at Weldon Railroad, June 12th, together with about two thousand others, including all of the 4th Vermont Regiment except Co. B. The prisoners were all taken to Libby Prison, Richmond, where every thing of value, including their blankets, over-coats and best clothing, was taken from them. They remained there three days and were then taken to Belle Isle, where they stayed two days and were then started for Andersonville by way of Lynchburg, Danville and Macon. They marched from Lynchburgh to Danville, seventy-five miles, in three days. They were kept at Andersonville five months, where they experienced all the horrors of that horribly loathsome place, about which so much has been said and written, and still much remains to be told. While there Mr. Burbank saw a rebel guard shoot a prisoner for asking him for a chew of tobacco. It was said that when a rebel guard for any reason killed a yankee prisoner he was given a thirty days' furlough. The rations there were a pint of cob-meal per day, without salt, and often this was of very poor quality. He was there when some of the prisoners dug out and were retaken by bloodhounds. Capt. Wirtz threatened to starve all the prisoners — thirty thousand — to death if they would not tell who the leaders were in digging out, and did withhold their pint of meal for three days, but finally, when he found none would tell, relented, and they had their miserable rations again. From Andersonville they were taken to Millen, thence to Savannah, from there to Blackshire, from there to Charleston, Florence, Goldsboro' and Wilmington, and were near the latter place when it was taken by our troops. They were taken again to Goldsboro', and on the last day of February, 1865, about a thousand of them were put upon a railroad train, run into our lines, and left near Wilmington. The prisoners thus returned were sent to Annapolis and given a thirty days' furlough. When Mr. Burbank was captured he weighed one hundred and fifty-five pounds, and

when he came home on furlough, four weeks after
he was released, he weighed less than a hundred
pounds. While at Andersonville our prisoners
died at the rate of one hundred and fifteen per
day on an average. He rejoined his regiment in
May and was mustered out in July, 1865. The
following August he was written to from Washington to give his experience at Andersonville, to
be used on the trial of Capt. Wirtz, and was also
sent for to appear there, but was unable to go. It
was several months before he recovered from the
effects of his sufferings. He tells his own story,
which would fill a volume, but is much like those
told by others who were so unfortunate as to fall
into rebel hands as prisoners of war. He now
lives in Claremont, and is an industrious and respected citizen.

CHARLES R. BARDWELL

Enlisted and was mustered into the 16th Vermont Reg't, for nine months, in August, 1862.
His regiment was in the battle of Gettysburg, in
July, 1863, soon after which it was mustered out.
He is a son of Charles Bardwell of Claremont.

HENRY S. BLANCHARD

Enlisted and was mustered into Co. A, 12th
Vermont, a nine months regiment, October 4, 1862.

Served his full time, and was mustered out July 14, 1863. The regiment was in no general battle. During the battle of Gettysburg it was engaged in guarding army teams near the scene of conflict. He returned home at the end of his term, and died of cancer, Dec. 19, 1867, at the age of twenty-three years. He was a son of the late Sylvanus Blanchard of Claremont, a good soldier and worthy young man.

ETHAN A. GILE

Enlisted and was mustered into the same regiment and served his full time.

WALLACE DANE

Enlisted and was mustered into Co. F, 4th Vermont Regiment, in the summer of 1861. He was in the seven days' retreat, became sick, and was in hospital at Philadelphia from June 1862, until January 1863, when he was discharged. He was a son of the late John Dane of Claremont, brother of Albert G. Dane of the 3d New-Hampshire Regiment, who died in Salisbury prison, and was twenty-three years old when he enlisted.

LEWIS HENRY DUTTON

Enlisted and was mustered into the 3d Vermont Volunteer Infantry Regiment in April, 1861, which was attached to the Army of the Potomac, and was appointed Orderly Sergeant. He was wounded severely in the foot at the battle of Fredericksburg, Dec. 13, 1862, and was discharged on account of his wound in March 1863. He was commissioned Lieutenant, but was not mustered on his commission. He is a son of Aaron Dutton of Claremont, and is now teaching at Manchester, N. H., and studying for the profession of law:

WILLIAM L. HURD

Enlisted and was mustered into Co. F, 3d Vermont Reg't, in June, 1861. He was killed at the battle of Lee's Mills, Va., April 16, 1862, where the Third, Fourth, Fifth and Sixth Vermont Regiments were engaged and acted bravely. While crossing Warwick Creek, which makes up from the James River, waist deep, to make a charge upon the rebel intrenchments, young Hurd was shot, and his body was never recovered. He was a brave soldier.

Captain CALVIN A. LAWS

Enlisted into the Woodstock, Vt., Light Infantry, which was mustered as Co. B, into the 12th Vermont Volunteer Infantry, Oct. 4, 1862. This was a nine months regiment, and was brigaded with four other Vermont nine months regiments, under command of Brig. Gen. Stoughton. He was with his regiment doing garrison, picket, and guard duty until May, 1863, when he was taken sick with fever, sent to hospital in Washington, and only rejoined the regiment when on its way home to be mustered out, in July, 1863. In May, 1864, he raised a company in Chicago, Ill., for one hundred days, of which he was commissioned Captain. His company was mustered into the 132d Illinois Regiment as Co. K, and did garrison duty at Columbus, Paducah, and Smithland, Ky., and went to St. Louis at the time of the rebel Gen. Price's raid. Returned to Chicago and was mustered out Oct. 17, 1864. He was a faithful soldier, good officer, and is a worthy young man. He is a son of Ebenezer Laws of Claremont.

BENJAMIN L. MEADER

Enlisted and was mustered into the 2d Vermont Regiment in April, 1861, for three years, when twenty-one years old; served to the end of the war and was mustered out with his regiment. He lived in Tunbridge, Vt., at the time he enlisted. He is a son of Nathan A. Meader of Claremont, and brother of Charles C. Meader, of the same regiment.

CHARLES C. MEADER

Enlisted and was mustered into the 2d Vermont Regiment, in April, 1861, for three years, when seventeen years old. He was wounded severely in the leg, and discharged in 1863. When he enlisted he lived at Newbury, Vt. He is a son of Nathan A. Meader of Claremont, and brother of Benj. L. Meader of the same regiment.

MASSACHUSETTS REGIMENTS.

OLIVER A. BOND

Enlisted and was mustered into Co. A, 47th Massachusetts, a nine months regiment, Sept. 28, 1862, and was discharged Oct. 8, 1863. This regiment was on guard and provost duty at New-Orleans during its entire term, and was in no battles. Harrison and George H. Waterman, brothers-in-law of Mr. Bond, were in the same regiment and company, and all were Corporals. Mr. Bond is a son of Daniel Bond of Claremont, and the Watermans lived here four or five years, being step-sons of Henry Hubbard.

SAMUEL STEPHEN CARLETON

Enlisted into the Fourth Battalion Massachusetts Rifles, for three months, in April, 1861, immediately after hearing of the assault on the 6th Massachusetts Regiment, in Baltimore. The men of this battalion soon reënlisted for three years, and was the nucleus of the 13th Massachusetts

Regiment. Carleton was wounded in the battle of Antietam, but not severely. He was in the battle at Chancellorsville, on the 4th of May, 1863, and in a skirmish with the enemy the next day, while helping a wounded man from the field, a minnie ball entered Carleton's left hip, passed clear through and came out on the other side, causing a compound fracture of the right hip bone. The splinters formed dead bone. and could not work out. He was taken prisoner, placed under a table out of doors where the rebel surgeons were amputating limbs of their wounded, where he was kept ten days, through he had as good care as they could give him. He was then paroled, placed in corps hospital, and afterward sent to Washington, where he remained until February, 1864. From there he was returned to Boston, and placed in hospital, and in June came home to Claremont. Here he laid upon his back, suffering beyond description. For ten or twelve months hopes were entertained of his recovery, when a diarrhea, from which he was suffering when he came here, set in and followed him until his death, Jan. 23, 1867. His wound never healed, but discharged continually, averaging more than a pint a day. He was a son of Stephen Carleton of Claremont, and brother of Elijah S. Carleton of the 5th Regiment, a patternmaker by trade, and twenty-one years old when he enlisted.

SAMUEL W. CHAPMAN

Enlisted and was mustered into Co. E, First Massachusetts Heavy Artillery, Aug. 7, 1864, for three years or during the war. He was taken prisoner before Richmond, Oct. 3, 1864, carried to Belle Isle, thence to Salisbury, N. C., and was there with John G. P. Putnam, Ard Scott, Albert G. Dane and George W. Constantine. Early in the following March he was paroled and sent to Annapolis, Md., and soon came home where he died April 5, 1865, from the effects of exposure and starvation while in prison. On his arrival home he was too feeble and his mind too much shattered to give a coherent account of himself or his sufferings. His experience was similar to that of John G. P. Putnam of the 3d New-Hampshire Regiment, given in the notice of him. He came from Manchester to Claremont, and married a sister of Ard Scott of the 3d New-Hampshire, and Henry Scott of the 4th Massachusetts Regiment.

HORACE W. COOK

Enlisted and was mustered into Co. F, 24th Massachusetts Reg't, in January, 1864, and served to the end of the war. He is a brother of Wendell R. and William W. Cook of the 5th New-Hampshire Reg't, and son of Wakefield Cook of Claremont.

FREDERIC WORTH GODDARD

Enlisted at Malden, Mass., in September, 1862, for nine months, and was mustered into Co. H, 44th Massachusetts Regiment, but was soon transferred to Co. B, 45th Massachusetts Volunteer Infantry. The regiment left Boston for Newburn, N. C., in November, 1862. Shortly after its arrival there he was detailed for duty in the Signal Corps, where he remained until the latter part of March, 1863, when he was returned to his regiment, and was with them in one slight skirmish at Gore Creek Bridge, North-Carolina, April 27th and 28th, 1863. The regiment was in no general engagement after his return to it, its service consisting of severe picket and patrol duty. The end of the term of the regiment found the men all debilitated by climate and unaccustomed exposure. They were embarked for Boston about June 20, 1863. Some died, and many were taken mortally ill on the passage. When they arrived at Boston, June 29, Mr. Goddard was among the very ill. In his delirium he thought to join the march through the streets of Boston, but could only be borne carefully to the Military Hospital in Pemberton Square, where, with a few of the home friends to watch him, he died July 3, 1863, while Gettysburg guns were marking the crisis of the rebellion, and only a few days before the end of his term of enlistment,— one of the unnumbered lost whose unnoticed sufferings and toils form always the material out of which military glory comes to the few. His remains were brought to Claremont, and, after impressive ceremonies, were interred in the family lot. He was the second son of Edward L. Goddard; was born in Claremont, Nov. 14, 1848; and was one of many young men who entered the army from purely patriotic motives, and gave their valuable lives for their country.

HENRY W. MACE

Enlisted and was mustered into the 53d Massachusetts nine months regiment, and served a little more than a year. He again enlisted for a hundred days, and spent the time in garrison duty. He is a son of Oliver Mace of Claremont, and now resides in Fitchburg, Mass.

THOMAS D. PARRISH

Enlisted and was mustered into Co. F, 26th Massachusetts Reg't, Sept. 18, 1861, going from

Claremont to Lawrence, Mass., for that purpose. He was in most of the battles where his regiment was engaged, but never received a wound. He reënlisted in January, 1864, was mustered out with his regiment, Sept. 1865, returned to Claremont, and is now at work here as a file-cutter. He is a brother of Lyman F., William E., and James C. Parrish, all of whom were good soldiers.

CHARLES C. STORY

Enlisted into the 6th Massachusetts Reg't at Washington, just after the assault by the mob in the streets of Baltimore in April, 1861. At the end of three months — the term for which the regiment enlisted — he returned to Boston with it and was mustered out. Story was one of Gen. Butler's body guard, when, on the 14th of May, 1861, with a strong force, he went from the Relay House to Baltimore, and marched through the streets of the city with music and banners, thus saying practically to the rebels, "Now attack us if you dare!" He is a printer, son of Francis B. and Olive G. Story, brother of Edward E. Story of the 6th New-Hampshire Regiment, and half brother of David H. Grannis of the 3d New-Hampshire Reg't.

HENRY SCOTT

Enlisted and was mustered into Co. H, 4th Massachusetts Regiment, in August, 1861, and went out with Gen. Banks' expedition. It was at New-Orleans, in the siege of Port Hudson, and in several battles. This was a nine months regiment, but remained out thirteen months. Mr. Scott was most of the time on duty at the Colonel's quarters. He is a brother of Sergeant Ard Scott of the 3d New-Hampshire Regiment, who died in Salisbury prison.

DENNIS TAYLOR

Enlisted under Capt. Austin, in April, 1861, for three months, and served out the term of his enlistment at Fort Constitution. He subsequently enlisted and served in the 5th Massachusetts Regiment.

HORACE A. TYRRELL

Enlisted in September, 1864, and was mustered into the 2d Massachusetts Cavalry. After being out a few months he was taken with chronic diarrhea, was discharged, and died on the way home. He was a son of Harmon Tyrrell of Claremont, and was less than seventeen years old when he enlisted.

REGIMENTS FROM OTHER STATES.

Captain JAMES E. AINSWORTH

Was Captain in the 12th Iowa Regiment, and participated in the battles of Fort Henry, Fort Donelson and Shiloh. He resigned on account of disability after about a year's service, and returned to his home at Dubuque. Is a son of the late Ralph Ainsworth of Claremont, and brother of Charles. H. Ainsworth.

Lieutenant C. EDWARD BINGHAM

Entered the military service in December, 1862. He was engaged in recruiting for the Second Regiment Rhode-Island Cavalry until February, 1863, when he was commissioned by the Governor of Rhode-Island, First Lieutenant Co. H, of that regiment, which joined Gen. Banks' expedition to New-Orleans, and was subsequently engaged in the Teche Campaign, Red River Expedition, and the siege of Port Hudson. In May, 1863, he was appointed Adjutant, which position he held until the following July, when the regiment, having been reduced to about three hundred men, was consolidated into a battalion, and the field and staff officers mustered out. Lieut. Bingham was offered a captaincy in the new battalion, which, on account of impaired health, he felt compelled to decline. He resigned and came home in a very feeble condition, caused by his arduous duties in field and camp, together with exposure in a southern climate, from which he did not recover under several months. He is a son of Charles M. Bingham of Claremont, and was a capable, efficient and brave officer.

GEORGE COLBY

Enlisted for three years and was mustered into the 24th Illinois Reg't, in July, 1861. He was in an engagement at Fredericksburg, Mo., thence went with his regiment to Fort Holt, opposite Cairo, Ill., and helped to plant the first guns there while being shelled by rebel gun boats. Afterward he went to Kentucky, and when on picket was shot at by a bushwhacker, the ball lodging in a tree just above his head. His regiment kept the front in the march from Bowling Green, Ky., to Huntsville, Ala., under Gen. O. M. Mitchell, and subsequently guarded sixty miles of the Memphis and Charleston railroad in the enemy's country.

He was in the fight at Perryville, Ky., with Gen. Bragg, under Gen. Rousseau, when one half his regiment was killed or wounded; and afterward. in the battles at Murfreesborough, Tenn., Chickamoga, Chattanooga, and Buzzard's Roost, and finished his term of enlistment as guard on the Louisville and Nashville railroad. In 1862 he was captured by Morgan, soon paroled, and subsequently exchanged. He reënlisted and served ten months in the 15th Kentucky regiment. He is a son of Ira Colby of Claremont, and now lives at West Union, Iowa.

JAMES B. FORD

Enlisted at Lewiston, Me., April 20, 1861, for three months, and was mustered into Co. K, First Maine Reg't, with which he served until the expiration of its term of enlistment and was mustered out. Soon after he enlisted at Fairfield, Me., for three years, and was mustered into Co. E, Seventh Maine Reg't, and was discharged for disability Sept. 26, 1861. He is a printer by trade, son of the late Rev. J. W. Ford, and brother of George E. Ford of the New-Hampshire Heavy Artillery, and Lieut. Charles P. Ford of the 75th New-York Regiment.

Lieutenant CHARLES P. FORD

Enlisted and was mustered into Co. I, 75th Reg't New-York Volunteers, in September, 1861. Appoint Sergeant, and was successively promoted to Second and First Lieutenant. He served with his regiment in the Department of the Gulf for nearly three years, when it was sent home to reënlist the old soldiers and fill up with new recruits, which, having been accomplished, the regiment went to Virginia, and soon after Lieut. Ford resigned. He is a son of the late Rev. J. W. Ford, and brother of James B. Ford, who served in the 1st and 7th Maine regiments, and George E. Ford of the New-Hampshire Heavy Artillery. He now lives in Auburn, N. Y.

CHARLES B. GRANDY

Enlisted and was mustered into the 62d Reg't New-York Volunteer Infantry, in May, 1861. He was taken down with typhoid fever in October following, and after a sickness of six days, died at Washington, and was buried with military honors by his company at Tenallytown grave yard. He was a son of the late Alpha Grandy of Claremont, and left home about two years before the breaking out of the rebellion, went to New-York city and was employed in the Fifth Avenue Hotel. He was the main support of a widowed mother, an invalid sister and younger brother. He is spoken of as an upright young man, a good and faithful soldier, and his death was lamented by the officers and men of his company. At the time of his death he was twenty-one years old.

GILES P. MARVIN,

In the autumn of 1861, when fifteen years old, entered the army as servant for Capt. George C. Starkweather of the 6th Reg't. In about three months Capt. Starkweather resigned, and young Marvin came home. The following May he made several attempts to enlist, but failed on account of his age. In May, 1863, when less than seventeen years old, he enlisted at New-Haven and was mustered into Co. F, First Connecticut Cavalry. His regiment was for nearly a year at Baltimore doing provost duty, after which it was attached to the Cavalry Corps under Gen. Sheridan, and Grant's Army of the James. The regiment was in the great battle of the Wilderness and lost five hundred men in killed, wounded, and taken prisoners, in twenty minutes, out of nine hundred who went into the fight. It was engaged in Wilson's raid on the Richmond and Danville railroad, during which young Marvin very narrowly escaped with his life.

He was in the battles of Barryville, Winchester, Fisher's Hill, Cedar Creek, Hatcher's Run, Five Forks, Harper's Ferry and Appomatox Court House, where Lee's surrender took place, and Marvin, with some other men of his company, escorted Gen. Grant to the field. He participated in twenty-three engagements, and yet returned home without having received a wound. He was mustered out in August, 1865; is a brother of Charles B. Marvin of the 9th New-Hampshire Reg't, and son of the late Giles P. Marvin of Claremont.

WILLIAM H. H. REDFIELD

Was drafted at Meriden, Conn., and mustered into the 16th Connecticut Reg't. He was wounded in the battle of the Wilderness, and also at Petersburg. He is a son of William Redfield of Claremont, and brother of Willis Redfield, of the 15th Connecticut regiment.

WILLIS REDFIELD

Enlisted in July, 1862, and was mustered into the 15th Connecticut Reg't. He died at Newburn, N. C., Oct. 11, 1864, of yellow fever, and was buried there. He was a son of William Redfield, and brother of William H. H. Redfield of the 16th Connecticut Reg't, and was nineteen years of age at the time of his death.

AUSTIN I. HURD

Enlisted in October, 1862, and served at head-quarters of the 16th New-Hampshire Regiment and in the postal service fourteen months. He enlisted for nine months, while a student at the Conference Seminary at Sanbornton Bridge. He is a son of Cyrus Hurd of Claremont, and brother of William L. Hurd of the 3d Vermont Regiment, who was killed at the battle of Lee's Mills, Va.

Doctor SAMUEL G. JARVIS

Was appointed by the War Department Examining Pension Surgeon for Sullivan county, in 1861, and, although he was entitled to a fee from each soldier examined, he freely gave his services to all. From the time of the breaking out of the rebellion to the close of the war, he gave his professional services to soldiers and their families, and in many other ways, by his influence and his means, encouraged enlistments and aided in putting down the rebellion.

ANSON M. SPERRY

Enlisted under Capt. Austin, for three months, in April, 1861, and declining to reënlist for three years was sent to Fort Constitution, where he served out his term of enlistment. His brother,

Nathaniel Sperry, served in the 1st Minnesota Regiment. They are sons of the late Bela J. Sperry.

SYLVESTER E. H. WAKEFIELD,

Charles F. Bacon, Anson M. Sperry and Ebenezer E. Cummings, enlisted under Capt. Austin, for three months, in April, 1861, went to Portsmouth, and there declining to reënlist for three years, were sent to Fort Constitution, where they served out their term of enlistment in performing garrison duty. Eight others, also, from Claremont, who went with them, subsequently entered other organizations and are appropriately noticed, while the four above named did not afterward enlist.

THE NAVY.

Doctor JEFFREY THORNTON ADAMS

Was appointed acting Assistant Surgeon in the navy in December, 1861, and was ordered to report to Com. Paulding, commanding the Navy-yard at New-York, which he did on the 16th of that month, and was assigned to duty as the only medical officer on board the United States armed ship Pursuit, which, in a few days, sailed on a cruise on the southern coast to watch blockade runners and rebels generally. In this cruise, it being ascertained that the rebel armed steamer Florida, a noted blockade runner, was skulking behind the islands and keys of the Gulf, volunteers from his ship were called for to man boats for her capture. Although professionally a non-combatant, and exempt from such service, yet feeling that as a surgeon he might be needed, he volunteered to go with one of the three armed row boats, on the enterprise. They were out rowing two days and three nights. On the second day they captured a small blockade runner, loaded with cotton, and one of the boats was detailed to secure the prize while the other two continued the search for the Florida. On the morning of the third day, before light, they discovered her at anchor forty miles from the fleet. They ranged along side of her with muffled oars, boarded and captured her after a sharp contest on deck. Dr. Adams was one of the first men to board the Florida. She was taken safely to the fleet and found to have on board a cargo of cotton valued at eighty thousand dollars. On this cruise the Pursuit also captured several other blockade runners and illicit rebel traders and smugglers, loaded with cotton, &c., and took them as prizes to the fleet. While on the coast Dr. Adams was assigned for a time to duty as Surgeon in charge of the United States Military Hospital at Key West. He remained in the Gulf service until maladies incident to a tropical climate so far impaired his health that he was compelled to ask leave of absence, and by advice of the fleet Surgeon, returned home. After some months at home, and having partially recovered his health, he returned to duty, and was ordered to a gun-boat on the Mississippi, but chronic diarrhea, which he had contracted in the Gulf, soon returned with malignant force, and he was obliged to seek a northern latitude. He resigned his position in the Navy and came home in

March, 1863. After a few months he so far recovered as to be able to accept the position of Assistant Surgeon in the United States Military Hospital at Brattleboro', Vt., where there was a large number of sick and wounded soldiers. At times he had charge of from one hundred to one hundred and fifty patients, beside performing other duties, to which he devoted himself with such zeal, tenderness and skill as to secure the confidence and esteem of officers and patients in the hospital. The Chaplain, Rev. J. A. Crawford, wrote of him — "He was a genial and most entertaining companion. He had seen much and read much, and one could listen to him long with great pleasure and profit. He was a great favorite with the men who were in his care. He did for them beyond his strength, and was tender and kind to a remarkable degree." This position he relinquished on account of the return of his old difficulty, in the winter of 1864-5, and again returned to his home in Claremont, where he died on the 17th of June, 1865. Dr. Adams was the eldest son of Joseph Thornton Adams of the Treasury Department, Washington, and was born in Boston, July 17, 1831. He was prepared for college at Derry Academy, and entered Harvard College at the age of fifteen, but on account of ill health did not complete the course.

He subsequently attended the Medical School at Castleton, Vt., where he graduated, receiving a diploma as physician and surgeon. He spent about two years in the practice of his profession in Minnesota, after which, in 1855, he returned to Claremont, opened an office, and remained in the practice of his profession until the breaking out of the rebellion, when he responded to the call of the country for his services.

GEORGE W. FITCH

Enlisted into the Navy as Carpenter, Nov. 22, 1861, and was assigned to the ship Morning Light. Discharged March 7, 1862, and came home to Claremont, and now resides here.

EMERY G. JUDKINS,

Appointed Acting Assistant Surgeon in the Navy in Nov. 1861, was assigned to the ship Morning Light. Resigned in April, 1862, and returned to Claremont. From here he moved to Waitsfield, Vt., where he died of diphtheria, on the 29th of June, 1863. His remains were brought to this town, where he was born, studied his profession, and practiced for several years, and were buried. He was a man of ability and many excellent qualities.

GEORGE E. JUDKINS

Was appointed Surgeon's Steward on board the ship Morning Light, in November, 1861. Resigned in April, 1862.

Corporal CHARLES C. PHILBROOK

Enlisted into the Naval service of the United States as a Marine, in August, 1861, and was assigned to the United States ship Pawnee. He left Fortress Monroe on the steamer Governor, in November, 1861. When two or three days out she encountered a severe storm and was wrecked. Those on board had a narrow escape from watery graves. After two days of suffering, all on board, except seven who undertook to save themselves in a small boat, were saved by the United States ship Sabine. He was in the Southern Blockading Expedition through the winter of 1861–62. He was appointed Corporal, and in July, 1864, promoted to Orderly Sergeant of the United States supply steamer Union. Served until the end of the war and was honorably discharged. He is a son of A. S. Philbrook of Claremont, and brother of Rev. Hiram Philbrook of Calais, Me., who was Chaplain of the 8th Maine regiment.

SUMMARY.

Whole number of volunteers from Claremont, 370
" " " drafted men who entered the army, 5
" " " " " " furnished substitutes, 74
" " killed in battle, 33
" " who died of wounds, 14
" " " " " disease, 20
" " " served to the end of the war, 85
Number of families who received aid from the Town and State, 173
Amount of Town and State aid furnished to families, $26,219.61

This summary includes all the Claremont soldiers who were connected with New-Hampshire, and other regiments whose history is known. Many reënlisted, while others served in more than one organization — some in three or four — which, with substitutes furnished and commutation paid by men who were drafted, make the whole number 449, of soldiers put down to the credit of the town during the war.

CLAREMONT'S QUOTA.

The enrollment in Claremont, in April, 1865, embracing all male citizens of the age of eighteen years, and under the age of forty-five years, liable to do military duty, was 413. The whole number who entered the Army and Navy from this town, from April, 1861, to April, 1865, was 449. This includes all enlistments — some of the men having enlisted two or more times — the drafted men who paid commutation or furnished substitutes, and those who entered the army. The quota required to be sent from each town in the State under all calls for troops, from July, 1863, was proportioned to the number of enrolled militia, as above. Claremont's quota was set down at 177, and she furnished 206 recruits, being an excess of 29 over what she was required to furnish.

LADIES' SOLDIERS' AID SOCIETIES.

Immediately after the assault upon Fort Sumter and the call of the President for seventy-five thousand volunteers, the ladies of Claremont manifested their zeal in the cause of their country by meeting at the house of Mrs. Susan J. Adams, to prepare bandages and other articles needed in army hospitals.

In May an urgent call came to the ladies for hospital stores and garments suitable for the sick and wounded. A notice was published in the village papers inviting the ladies to meet in Fraternity Hall. At the appointed time a large number assembled. The meeting was called to order by Miss Elizabeth Sprague. Remarks were made urging the importance of organized and earnest effort to minister to the comfort of sick and wounded soldiers, and to give to our men articles of clothing not furnished them by the Government.

A society called the Ladies' Union Sewing Circle was organized by the choice of the following officers: Mrs. M. A. Metcalf, President; Mrs. Edward L. Goddard, Vice-President; Miss Elizabeth Sprague, Secretary and Treasurer; Mrs. Obed D. Barnes, Mrs. Otis F. R. Waite, Mrs. Lewis Perry, Mrs. Charles H. Eastman, Mrs. Edward L. Goddard, and Mrs. Mary A. Blanchard, committee to have especial care and direction of the work.

This society met at Fraternity Hall daily. The work at first was upon flannel garments and other articles for the men enlisted by Capt. William P. Austin, a large portion of whom belonged in Claremont. Each man was furnished by this society with a pair of woolen drawers, undershirt, towels, pocket-handkerchiefs, woolen socks, pin-flat, and needle-book well filled with useful articles. By special contribution they raised $75 for rubber blankets, $8.30 for havelocks, and $13.29 for extra pairs of woolen hose.

The ladies kept at work as well at home as at their stated meetings, throughout the summer, for soldiers and hospitals. In September, Charles H. Long enlisted a company of one hundred men for the Fifth Regiment, all belonging in Claremont and vicinity, and each was furnished with bed-sack, towels, handkerchiefs and woolen hose.

Auxiliary Sanitary Commission.

Early in October, 1861, the United States Sanitary Commission sent an appeal to the ladies of Claremont to organize an Auxiliary Sanitary Commission, in order the better to systematize their labors and the manner of sending forward and appropriating to their proper uses the fruits of their liberality and labor. In response to a call the citizens met at Fraternity Hall on the 11th of October for this purpose. Simeon Ide, Thomas J. Harris, Joseph Weber, Mrs. Edward L. Goddard, Mrs. M. A. Metcalf and Mrs. Charles H. Eastman were appointed a committee to prepare and report at a subsequent meeting a plan of organization. Mrs. Obed D. Barnes, Miss Jane W. Prentiss, and Mrs. James Goodwin, were appointed a committee to canvass the town and secure the coöperation of all loyal women in this movement.

An adjourned meeting was held on the 16th of October, when the committee submitted a plan of organization, making every lady in town, who would pay into the treasury one dollar, a member, and proposed the following list of officers, which report was adopted: Simeon Ide, President; Mrs. Samuel P. Fiske and Mrs. Leonard P. Fisher, Vice-

Presidents; Thomas J. Harris, Treasurer; Cyrenus S. Parkhurst, Secretary; Edward L. Goddard, Frederick T. Kidder, Arthur Chase, Mrs. M. A. Metcalf, Mrs. G. W. Lewis, Mrs. Obed D. Barnes, Mrs. Edward L. Goddard, Mrs. Charles H. Eastman, and Mrs. Jotham G. Allds, Directors.

The Directors appointed Mrs. Lewis Perry, Miss Marion Richards, Mrs. Francis Whitcomb, Miss Diantha Sargent, Miss Alice Jones, Mrs. James Goodwin, Mrs. James Brickett, Mrs. Otis F. R. Waite, Mrs. Stephen F. Rossiter, Mrs. David F. Tutherly, Miss Stella Wallingford, Miss E. M. Bond, Mrs. Albert O. Hammond, Mrs. Freeman S. Chellis, Mrs. Amos D. Johnson, Mrs. Robert Bunnel, Mrs. Anson S. Barstow, Mrs. George W. Lewis, and Miss Isabella D. Rice, to solicit money, hospital stores — such as preserves, jellies, pickles, etc., or clothing — to fill a box which the society wished to send forward.

For a time this organization received the active coöperation of the gentlemen holding the principal offices, after which they seemed occupied with other matters, and early in the winter of 1861 the ladies took the management and funds of the society, Mrs. Samuel P. Fiske acting as President, and Mrs. Edward L. Goddard as Secretary and Treasurer.

The sewing circle was a Union Sewing Circle in the fullest acceptation of the term. Love of country, love for the brave and noble soldiers who left their homes to fight our battles, to suffer and die in prison or hospital, helped these patriotic women to surmount every obstacle and forget all opposition and discouragement.

A few ladies of Unity sent valuable contributions which were forwarded in the first boxes sent to Washington.

The meetings were frequent, well attended, seemed to be pervaded by a solemn sense of the importance of the utmost diligence in the performance of the work in hand, and pleasant to all interested in their object. Many ladies, whose names do not appear as having an especial charge, were among the most active and efficient workers.

Among the gentlemen in town most active and enthusiastic in aiding the ladies in their work, encouraging enlistments and helping soldiers and their families, was Rt. Rev. Carlton Chase, Bishop of the Diocese of New-Hampshire. He opened his house to the ladies, attended and addressed public meetings, and in other ways showed how much he had the cause of the country at heart.

The ladies engaged in this Society, enlisted for the war, nor did they cease their efforts until Richmond was taken and the rebel armies had surrendered. During the existence of this Auxiliary Society they sent thirty-three large boxes to the United States Sanitary Commission Rooms in Washington and Boston, containing the following articles: 153 pairs woolen drawers, 195 woolen shirts, 373 cotton shirts, 29 pairs cotton drawers, 1029 towels, 901 handkerchiefs, 84 needle books, 624 pairs woolen hose, 221 woolen blankets, 333 quilts, 169 sheets, 244 pairs mittens, 39 comfort bags, 45 vests, 59 pillow sacks, 139 bed sacks, 261 pillows, 241 pillow-cases, 198 pairs slippers, 189 dressing gowns, 51 havelocks, 2 collars, 1 military overcoat, 1 military dress coat, 1 pair military pants, 1 blouse, 1 linen jacket, together with large quantities of dried and canned fruits, pickles, bandages, lint, linen and cotton pieces, 75 quarts of wines and 50 pounds of corn starch, books and other reading matter, all of which was most generously given by the friends of the soldier in every part of the town. They also sent to the Boston and Baltimore Fairs for the benefit of the soldiers, about one hundred and fifty dollars' worth of fancy articles, all of which were contributed by the ladies of this Society.

The Society received from its members and other individuals about twelve hundred dollars — four hundred dollars of which was realized from exhibitions, festivals and concerts. When they closed their labors in the spring of 1865, there remained in the treasury one hundred and sixty dollars, which was placed at interest, and is to be appropriated, with what has been and may be voted by the town and obtained from other sources, for the erection of a monument in commemoration of our brave soldiers who gave their lives for their country when she needed such noble sacrifice.

At the commencement of the war the ladies of West Claremont formed themselves into a working band for the soldiers, and met together occasionally for work, though much was done at their homes. Large numbers of articles were sent to their destination during the first few months, through the Society at the village, after which they sent the articles of their benevolence and industry direct to Washington. As no officers were chosen, no record of the money expended was kept for any length of time. The money used and articles given were from residents at West Claremont, except fifty dollars from the Sanitary Commission in the village, in the winter of 1864-65, placed in the hands of Mrs. Wyllys Redfield, and expended for materials which were made up by the ladies. During the war not less than eight or ten barrels and boxes, filled with quilts, shirts, dressing-gowns, socks, dried fruits, jellies, wines, and many other articles, were sent by the ladies of West Claremont.

It is refreshing to remember, and a pleasure to record the earnestness and zeal manifested by the ladies of Claremont from the time of the commencement to the close of the war. They attended the meetings to consider the condition of the country; worked almost without intermission for the men in field and hospital; visited and consoled those whose husbands, sons, brothers and friends had enlisted, and in other ways showed that they had the cause of the country and those who went forth to fight for it near their hearts. Nor was this confined to any class, sect or neighborhood. It gave strength to the arms and courage to the hearts of the men, and comfort and material aid to their families. When the men went forth to the field they felt and knew that they left behind them wives, mothers, sisters and friends whose frequent and earnest prayers ascended to heaven for their safety, complete success and speedy return.

THANKSGIVING TO SOLDIERS' FAMILIES.

In November, 1864, Charles M. Bingham, Nathaniel Tolles, Otis F. R. Waite, Samuel G. Jarvis and Walter H. Smith, were chosen a committee to collect contributions and distribute to families of soldiers, and others in town who were considered needy, provisions for Thanksgiving. Citizens cheerfully contributed from their stores what was valued in cash at $30.31, and in money $120.45 — making a total of $150.76. The money received was carefully expended for provisions, which were distributed to one hundred and three families according as the committee judged of their several needs. The articles carried to the different dwellings consisted of 150 chickens, 75 roasters of beef, weighing from 7 to 14 pounds each, several pieces of fresh pork, a large quantity of butter, cheese, vegetables, groceries, &c.

SOLDIERS' MONUMENT.

At the annual town meeting in March, 1867, it was voted to appropriate one thousand dollars for the erection of a Monument to those Claremont men who had been killed in battle or died in the army in the War of the Rebellion, on condition that five hundred dollars should be raised by subscription or otherwise for the same purpose. The Ladies' Sanitary Commission appropriated the funds — about one hundred and sixty dollars — which they had on hand at the close of the war, to this object; and the Committee of Arrangements for the Fourth of July Celebration in 1865, also appropriated about fifty dollars which they had after paying expenses. In addition to this the ladies obtained in subscriptions, not exceeding one dollar each, a sufficient amount to secure the town appropriation, and these several sums, except the thousand dollars voted by the town, were placed at interest. At the annual town meeting in March, 1868, the further sum of two thousand dollars was voted for this object, provided that one thousand dollars should be raised by contribution or otherwise. At the same meeting Samuel P. Fiske, Benjamin P. Gilman, Edward L. Goddard, Charles H. Long and John L. Farwell, were chosen a committee to have the matter in charge.

Fred. A. Briggs, Oliver A. Bond, Hosea W. Parker, A. George Boothe, William P. Farwell, James A. Cowles, Austin C. Chase, and some others, assisted by several young ladies, gave two very creditable dramatic exhibitions the first week in August, 1868, in aid of the Soldiers' Monument fund. A string band, extemporized for the occasion, and under the joint leadership of Messrs. George W. Wait of this town, and Henry A. Christie of Christie and Wedger's Band, Boston, who has his home in Claremont, furnished some excellent music and contributed very much to the entertainment. The receipts from this source were about one hundred and fifty dollars.

The committee have agreed to erect the monument on the Park. It is to be a granite pedestal surmounted by a bronze statue of an infantry volunteer— a design eminently appropriate— to be furnished by Martin Millmore of Boston. It is hoped that at no distant day this work, in commemoration of the noble and patriotic deeds of those brave Claremont men who laid their lives upon the altar of their country, will be properly completed, and that in other ways the people will manifest their affectionate remembrance of them.

www.ingramcontent.com/pod-product-compliance
Lightning Source LLC
Chambersburg PA
CBHW032042230426
43672CB00009B/1443